SHORT CUTS

INTRODUCTIONS TO FILM STUDIES

OTHER TITLES IN THE SHORT CUTS SERIES

MELODRAMA

GENRE, STYLE, SENSIBILITY

JOHN MERCER and MARTIN SHINGLER

WALLFLOWER

LONDON and NEW YORK

A Wallflower Press Book
Published by
Columbia University Press
Publishers Since 1893
New York • Chichester, West Sussex
cup.columbia.edu

Wallflower Press® is a registered trademark of Columbia University Press

Cataloging-in-Publication Data is available from the Library of Congress

ISBN 978-1-904764-02-1 (pbk.)
ISBN 978-0-231-50306-8 (e-book)

Book and cover design: Rob Bowden Design
Cover image: *Written on the Wind* (1956), Universal International Pictures

CONTENTS

ACKNOWLEDGEMENTS

Martin Shingler
This is a book I have been itching to write ever since I completed my under-graduate dissertation on the Hollywood family melodrama, so my first debt of gratitude is to my original film tutors, in particular Roger Powell and Peter Packer. It was this initial, tentative exploration of melodrama that led me to Thomas Elsaesser, with whom I studied for my Masters degree. His dedication to the study of film encouraged me to begin my PhD, and I continue to draw inspiration from his work and confidence from his support. My third debt is to the late Irving Rapper who, a few years before his death at the age of 101, generously talked to me over the telephone, from his bed in a New York apartment, about his life and work. I learnt then how much sensitivity and sheer humanity lay behind *Now, Voyager*, the film that had fired my imagination and initiated my earliest investigations into Hollywood melodrama. I am also indebted to all my colleagues in the Media Studies department at Staffordshire University for covering my teaching commitments during intensive periods of writing. I am particularly grateful to my good friend Ulrike Sieglohr, for the time and effort taken to read through drafts of my chapters and for all her sensible and practical suggestions for improvements. Likewise, Christine Gledhill, whose critical work has enabled me to formulate many of the ideas set down here, has also provided invaluable help, clarifying issues and concerns. The inspiration of her writing, her teaching, her enthusiasm for research and new ways of thinking, her energy and vision, not forgetting her friendship – all these have been vital, stimulating and rewarding. To Simon I owe the space to work in peace, for the treats and rewards in between, for listening to all my ideas when only half-baked and setting me back on course when straying into uncertain territory or simply failing to make sense. My final debt is to my co-writer John, for inviting me to be part of this project, for constant encouragement without pressure, for taking up the reins and getting the whole enterprise organised and ensuring we made good use of our time, for taking my many and varied concerns on board without hesitation or objection and, most of all, for being such good fun to work with.
To my father who always cries at The Sound of Music and my mother who saves her tears for real life.

John Mercer

I would like to thank my colleagues in the Arts and Media department at BCUC for their encouragement and ceaseless energy. I would particularly like to thank Ruth Gunstone, Alison Tedman and Lois Drawmer for their friendship and good humour that make my work such a pleasure. I would also like to thank my students whose own efforts to grapple with the difficult ideas discussed here and often stimulating observations and insights have helped shape the structure of this study. Like Martin, I would also like to extend my gratitude to Christine Gledhill who has been an instrumental figure both in the shaping of many of the ideas that this book deals with, and at a more personal level, for giving me my first opportunities to pursue a career as a film scholar. Thanks also to Martin, whose friendship, enthusiasm and expertise has made the completion of this study possible. Finally thanks to Trevor for his years of love, support and endless patience.

I dedicate this book to the memory of my grandparents, Bob and Mabel Nicholson, whose enthusiasm for cinema inspired my own fascinations at an early age. I love and miss you both.

INTRODUCTION

When, in 1971, retired Hollywood director Douglas Sirk gave an interview to Jon Halliday at his home in Switzerland, he could hardly have imagined the effect that his comments concerning the films that he made during his years as a contract director at Universal were to have on a succession of young filmmakers and on the emerging discipline of films studies. Sirk's identification of several of his films as 'melodramas' in effect initiated a debate around Hollywood cinema of the 1950s and its representation of the trials and tribulations of family life that has evolved into the identification of a broad category of cinema, one that often deals with highly-charged emotional issues, characterised by an extravagantly dramatic register and frequently by an overtly emotional mode of address.

Melodrama, however one might understand the term, always has the ability to provoke strong emotions in audiences, from tears of sorrow and identification, to derisive laughter. These powerful and contradictory responses are duplicated, to a greater or lesser degree, in the debates that have circulated amongst film scholars about what constitutes melodrama in cinema, its function as a genre, a filmic style or an expressive code. The melodrama debate that commences at the start of the 1970s includes some of the most complicated and difficult ideas in Film Studies and engages with almost all of the key theoretical ideas within the discipline, from questions of genre and authorship, to issues surrounding representation, aesthetics and the ideological function of cinema.

The challenge of this book, then, is to organise a range of, often conflicting, critical responses to the subject of melodrama into a coherent structure as an introduction to this complex area of film theory. Readers should be aware that this book offers no single definition of what melodrama is. Rather it should be understood as offering an overview of the various ways in which film theorists have made use of melodrama as a term and its associated debates to discuss key issues such as authorship, genre, ideology, cinematic *mise-en-scène*, feminism, psychoanalysis, reception and affect.

In the first chapter we discuss the relationship between melodrama and the study of genre in cinema. Melodrama, like film noir, is a critical category that emerges as a consequence of the identification of a range of films (largely made in the 1940s and 1950s) which use the family and the social position of women as their narrative focus. Film scholars, most notably Thomas Elsaesser, have argued that these texts constitute a specific generic category: the family melodrama, a genre that exposes the tensions and contradictions that lie beneath the surface of post-war suburban American life.

We note that Elsaesser's identification of the family melodrama and the intervention of feminist film theorists and their interests in the woman's film was to initiate a range of critical attempts to either define or reject melodrama as a genre. Through an analysis of early cinematic melodrama – in particular D. W. Griffith's *Broken Blossoms* (1919), the woman's film of the Classical Hollywood period *Stellas Dallas* (King Vidor, 1937) and the 1950s family melodrama, *Rebel Without a Cause* (Nicholas Ray, 1950) – we identify the ways in which this broad range of examples can be regarded as belonging to a similar generic category.

In chapter two we discuss the relationship between melodrama and cinematic style. The work of Elsaesser, Fred Camper, Paul Willemen, Laura Mulvey and Geoffrey Nowell-Smith not only identifies the family melodrama, but also notes that the films belonging to this generic category are often distinguished by a peculiarly exaggerated and excessive style. The principle exponent of this style was the director Douglas Sirk, whose lavish dramas made for Universal Studios in the mid 1950s were marked by a highly expressive *mise-en-scène* in which colour, gesture, costume, music, lighting and camera-work all conspired to produce cinematic texts rich with suppressed meaning and significance. Due to the investigations of this group of theorists, any discussion of cinematic melodrama inevitably returns to Douglas Sirk and what is seen as his distinctive filmic style and aesthetic vision. We thus note the emergence of this preoccupation with Sirk's techniques and its connections to wider debates within Film Studies. The elements of Sirk's style are identified through case study examples and in particular a thematic reading of *All That Heaven Allows* (1955). Sirk was to become a key figure, not just for film theorists, but also for successive generations of filmmakers and his stylistic influences are discussed in the work of both Rainer Werner Fassbinder and in the cinema of the contemporary director Todd Haynes.

The final chapter deals with more recent approaches to the question of melodrama and cinema. Here we discuss melodrama in more fluid terms as a sensibility that both informs an audience's reception of a range of texts marked by their heightened emotionality and very direct appeal to the sentiments and as an expressive code or mode that first emerged in the theatre of the eighteenth and nineteenth centuries and has evolved and mutated into a highly dramatic form of cinematic address. We discuss Christine Gledhill's interventions in the melodrama debate and note the extent to which her suggestion that melodrama should be regarded as a mode enables discussion around melodrama to continue to be relevant. We also look at the ways in which this broader understanding of melo-drama makes it possible to identify a melodramatic sensibility in a diverse range of cinematic texts, including the action movie for example, as well as cinema made for and by gay men.

We have included a short annotated reading list including the most useful texts that discuss melodrama and cinema that are currently in print as well as a wider bibliography and a thematic filmography that identifies a broader range of examples than space will allow in this introduction to the subject.

1   GENRE

Even though melodrama has been a significant feature of cinema from the very beginning, it is only since the early 1970s that film scholarship has paid it serious attention. During the 1970s and 1980s, melodrama acquired a new status amongst film historians, theorists and critics, many of whom sought to define the basic thematic and stylistic features of the form, its antecedents and evolution on screen, its influence, appeal and its ideology. In the process, melodrama was not only defined and demarcated as a genre but also refined and its boundaries redrawn. Within Film Studies, opinion has differed over what the term 'melodrama' means, what it designates, what kinds of films can have this term applied to them.

The identification of melodrama as a genre emerged in the wake of a range of theoretical and methodological approaches being adopted within Film Studies: most notably, Neo-Marxism, psychoanalysis and feminism. In other words, melodrama became a primary focus of academic interest at a time when ideology, psychoanalysis and gender were the most hotly debated issues within Film Studies, providing opportunities for all of these to be pursued within a single cinematic form. However, what became 'melodrama' within Film Studies was never a *single cinematic form* but rather a hybrid of various sub-genres and film cycles. Films were drawn into the category of 'melodrama' from such areas of cinema as romantic drama, historical costume drama, psychological thrillers, gothic thrillers, women's weepies, domestic dramas, juvenile delinquency films, crime thrillers, and so on. Whilst 'melodrama' became a convenient umbrella term that could embrace all of these types of movie, the term was simultaneously used and applied to a range of specific sub-genres, primarily the 'family melodrama' and the 'maternal melodrama'. For some scholars, the term 'melo-drama' also became synonymous with the Woman's Film. Not surprisingly, this has led to both confusion and argument on the part of film scholars. In the course of examining the notion of melodrama as a genre, we shall encounter some of the ambiguities and contradictions that have arisen within Film Studies and note some of the ways in which melodrama has been understood in very different terms by different film theorists.

Determining the genre

Genre has played an important role in the historical development of mainstream cinema. It is also an important concept within Film Studies. As a concept, genre allows a film to be identified as belonging to a larger body of work with shared themes, styles, attitudes and values. It is also an approach to film study or film history that emphasises the role of the audience in the creation of a series of related films. The development of a specific genre or 'film cycle' requires a consistently positive audience response to its style and content, its associated stars, directors, plots, props and settings. Genre studies have tended to recognise the crucial role played by audiences in the commercial film industry. Such studies tend to reveal how a film that had received a favourable audience response spawned a series of imitations or 'variations on a theme'. This series of films is then seen to have resulted in either a 'cycle' of films over a specific period of time (say, several years), for example the Universal Horror films of the 1930s, or to a more diverse body of cinema over a much longer time-scale (say, several decades), involving noticeable shifts in style or content, for example the western.

Genres are not just created by audiences and film companies however; critics and historians play a major role in recognising and, on occasion, *determining* groupings of films and designating them a specific generic category. This was most famously the case with 'film noir', a genre widely recognised today within both Film Studies and the film industry itself. This was a term that had little meaning during the 1940s, the period when most films now labelled 'film noir' were being made and shown. The French film critic Nino Frank first used the term in 1946 to describe a number of Hollywood films made during the Second World War: *The Maltese Falcon* (John Huston, 1941), *Murder My Sweet* (Edward Dmytryck, 1944), *Double Indemnity* (Billy Wilder, 1944), *Laura* (Otto Preminger, 1944) and *The Woman in the Window* (Fritz Lang, 1944). The term was subsequently taken

5

up and repeatedly used by critics writing for the French film journal *Cahiers du cinéma* during the 1950s. By the end of the 1960s, the term 'film noir' was being used widely within Anglo-American film criticism and, since the 1970s, has circulated even more widely within the international film industry and journalism (see Krutnik 1991).

The history of the term 'melodrama' is similar but also significantly different from that of film noir. It is similar in that what came in the 1980s and 1990s to be understood as melodrama is largely the result of the work of film critics and historians long after the films themselves had been made. It is significantly different in that the term 'melodrama' was widely used within the film industry and film journalism prior to its adoption by critics and historians. In fact, it was used to describe something very different to what the term came to mean during the 1970s. Steve Neale (1993) suggests that as far as the American film companies were concerned, from c.1910 to 1970 the term 'melodrama' meant action thrillers with fast-paced narratives, episodic story-lines featuring violence, suspense and death-defying stunts. Dastardly villains, heroines in peril and daring adventurous heroes populated these films, their actions speaking louder than their words. Cowboy films, gangster films, crime thrillers and horror movies were typically labelled 'melodramas' in the trade press. In fact, many of the films subsequently referred to as 'film noir' were described as 'melodramas' or 'mellers' (the shortened, slang version). Although one or two of these found their way into the Film Studies' version of 'melodrama' – most notably, *Mildred Pierce* (Michael Curtiz, 1945) – the vast bulk of the films previously labelled 'melodrama' by the industry have been excluded in order to make way for a strikingly different set of films. Ironically, what Film Studies has come to regard as 'melodrama' since 1970 are films with more words than action, inactive male protagonists, active and even domineering female characters, and anything but clear-cut and easily identifiable villains. In other words, the conception of 'melodrama' arrived at by film scholars after 1970 is almost diametrically opposed to the conception of 'melodrama' that circulated in the American film industry trade press in an earlier period. It is, however, the Film Studies' version of 'melodrama' that is now in general circulation, having been adopted by Hollywood filmmakers, reviewers and journalists since the 1970s. Meanwhile, those films once described as 'melodrama' by various sections of the film industry have come to be re-assigned under headings such as 'film noir', the 'western', 'suspense thriller' and 'horror movie.'

Constructing film melodrama's history

Film Studies has defined 'melodrama' in both broad and narrow terms. At its most general level, film scholars define it as a dramatic narrative with musical accompaniment to mark or punctuate the emotional effects, understanding the word to mean, literally, 'melos' (music) + 'drama'. Film scholarship has traced its history to a time before cinema, to eighteenth-century theatre and literature: for instance, the sentimental novels and plays of Jean-Jacques Rousseau. The best explanation of this historical development can be found in Christine Gledhill's essay 'The Melodramatic Field: An Investigation', which forms the introduction to her book *Home is Where the Heart Is: Studies in Melodrama and the Woman's Film* (1987: 14–22). As Gledhill and others have explained, melodrama emerged onto the stage as a new theatrical genre combining elements of both comedy and tragedy. At the level of pure entertainment, melodrama established notoriety through its astonishing twists and turns of fate, suspense, disaster and tragedy, its last-minute rescues and its happy endings. Whilst many of its themes were derived from morality plays, folk-tales and songs, stylistically it drew upon the conventions of pantomime and vaudeville. A key feature was its dependence upon an established system of non-verbal signs, gesture, *mise-en-scène* (sets, props, costumes and lighting) and music. The themes and style of this highly popular theatrical form proved eminently suitable for adaptation to the new cinematic medium, providing an obvious appeal for filmmakers seeking the widest and largest possible audience for their new product. Indeed, early American films drew heavily upon theatrical melodramas, especially after 1910 when, due to the introduction of four-reel films, more elaborate narratives were possible. One of the pioneering figures of early American cinema, D. W. Griffith, was quick to note the cinematic possibilities of an aesthetic dominated by action, spectacle, convoluted narratives and externalised emotions. *Birth of a Nation* (1915), *Broken Blossoms* (1919), *Way Down East* (1920) and *Orphans of the Storm* (1922) are all examples of the adoption of melodrama to the screen.[1] The fact that silent films relied upon live musical accompaniment for punctuation, was yet another reason behind early cinema's adoption of melodrama. In the absence of spoken dialogue, it was necessary for directors to develop a subtle, yet precise, formal visual language, one that could compensate for the expressive potency of the spoken word. Silent cinema, in its effort to engage and entertain, had good reason to be melodramatic but so too did sound cinema after 1927. Hence the development of a range of sub-genres, such as the Crime Melodrama – for example, *The Public Enemy* (William Wellman, 1931) – the Romantic Melodrama – *Camille* (George Cukor, 1936) – and the Maternal Melodrama – *Stella Dallas* (King Vidor, 1937). Melodrama not only survived the coming of sound but went on to flourish in Hollywood, particularly in the 1940s and 1950s. Films by William Wyler (*The Little Foxes*, 1941), Jean Negulesco (*Humoresque*, 1946), Max Ophüls (*Letter From an Unknown Woman*, 1948), Douglas Sirk (*Magnificent Obsession*, 1954), Nicholas Ray (*Rebel Without a Cause*, 1955) and Vincente Minnelli (*Home From the Hill*, 1959) testify to the success and pre-eminence of melodrama throughout this period. In short, melodrama has sustained a prominent position within Hollywood through-out its history. Its innate ability to engage, stimulate and entertain its audi-ence, to tears of joy and sadness, has ensured its longevity.

Film Studies' standard account of melodrama

Such a long and varied history has meant that the term 'melodrama' can be (and has been) applied to a large and diverse body of film spanning vir-tually every decade of filmmaking history and to different continents and cultures: American, European (for example, Gainsborough Melodrama) and Eastern (as with Hindi cinema).[2] Of course, such wide application and such a diversity of forms of cinema designated 'melodrama' reduces the term's critical value. What, after all, can be the value of a label that can be attached to so many different types of film? This was an issue that con-fronted film scholars in the early 1970s when the first steps towards inves-tigating melodrama as a genre were taken. Hence the following quotation from David Morse:

> In general, melodrama is a term of little critical value; it has been so corrupted in common usage that to give it a more specific field of reference is a task which almost verges on the impossible. On the other hand, it ought to be attempted because of the important role that melodrama has played in American culture and because of the influence it has exercised over the American cinema. (1972: 16–17)

Since the above comment appeared in print, much has been done to both affirm the critical reputation of melodrama and to determine a significant and identifiable genre worthy of study. Several of the first film scholars to undertake work on melodrama in the early 1970s sought to narrow the field of enquiry to a more limited and cohesive body of films. Consequently, the field became focused on a group of films made and released in the United States during the 1950s and directed by a relatively small selection of directors: chiefly, Douglas Sirk and Vincente Minnelli. This produced a more coherent field of investigation, a more distinctive canon of films with much greater consistency in terms of visual style, thematic content, performance and ideology. From this emerged what appeared to be the ultimate form of melodrama: the *Hollywood Family Melodrama*. In much the same way that film scholars had defined and demarcated the genre of the 'western', film theorists and historians identified the constituent features of the Hollywood family melodrama, providing a credible form of generic categorisation that enabled melodrama to be studied as a genre. The pioneering work of Thomas Elsaesser (1972) played a key role in this respect. He is commonly held to have been the first film critic to use the term 'family melodrama' and also to take it, implicitly at least, as the ultimate form of film melodrama. Certainly, many film scholars subsequently assumed that his comments regarding the Hollywood family melodrama were applicable to Hollywood melodrama more generally. Many certainly went on to adopt this approach in their own work: most notably, Geoffrey Nowell-Smith (1977), Laura Mulvey (1977/78) and Chuck Kleinhans (1978).

By the 1980s, a general understanding of what constituted the genre of the Hollywood family melodrama had been reached and a basic model formulated. This is most clearly demonstrated by Thomas Schatz's inclusion of a chapter on the family melodrama in his book *Hollywood Genres* (1981) alongside chapters on the western, the gangster film, the hard-boiled detective film, screwball comedy and the musical. In many ways, Schatz's project was the consolidation of the research that had been carried out by a range of genre critics, theorists and historians, each of these genres having previously been well-researched and critically established by this time. His incorporation of a chapter on the family melodrama indicates that, for Schatz at least, by the early 1980s the family melodrama had the same kind of generic status within Film Studies as the western and the gangster film.

For his chapter on the Hollywood family melodrama, Schatz set out what appeared to be a clear and coherent history from the silent era to 1960. This comprised of 1920s films by D. W. Griffith, 1930s films by Frank Borzage and John Stahl and 1940s films by Max Ophüls, Vincente Minnelli and Douglas Sirk. However, Schatz concentrated primarily on the 1950s, providing a list of family melodramas from 1954 to 1960. This list was dominated by the films of Sirk and Minnelli. This included Sirk's *Magnificent Obsession* (1954), *All That Heaven Allows* (1955), *Written on the Wind* (1956), *There's Always Tomorrow* (1956), *The Tarnished Angels* (1958) and *Imitation of Life* (1959). It also included Minnelli's *The Cobweb* (1955), *Tea and Sympathy* (1956), *Some Came Running* (1959) and *Home From the Hill* (1960). Together, the films of Sirk and Minnelli made up almost half the films on the list. The remainder was constituted by such films as Nicholas Ray's *Rebel Without a Cause* (1955) and *Bigger Than Life* (1956), Mark Robson's *Peyton Place* (1957) and *From the Terrace* (1960), Gordon Douglas' *Young at Heart* (1954), Elia Kazan's *East of Eden* (1955), Joshua Logan's *Picnic* (1956), George Stevens' *Giant* (1956) and Richard Brooks' *Cat on a Hot Tin Roof* (1958). Lesser-known films were also included, for instance *The Long Hot Summer* (Martin Ritt, 1956), *Too Much, Too Soon* (Art Napoleon, 1958), *A Summer Place* (Delmer Davies, 1959) and *The Bramble Bush* (Daniel Petrie, 1960). Schatz then subdivided this list of films into a number of discreet sub-genres or variants:

i)   the widow-lover melodramas, e.g., *All That Heaven Allows, Peyton Place, A Summer Place* and *Imitation of Life*
ii) the aristocratic family melodramas, e.g. *Written on the Wind, The Long Hot Summer, Giant, Cat on a Hot Tin Roof, From the Terrace* and *Home From the Hill*
iii) the male weepies, e.g., *Rebel Without a Cause, Tea and Sympathy, Bigger Than Life, East of Eden* and *The Cobweb*

Schatz also revealed that many of these films included a number of major themes and character-types, most notably:

i)   the 'intruder-redeemer' figure
ii) the search for the ideal husband/lover/father by anxious off-spring
iii) the household as the locus of social interaction
iv) the ambiguous function of marriage (as simultaneously sexually liberating and socially restricting)

Schatz's descriptions of these films also noted the recurrence of:

i)   victimised heroes
ii) conflict between the generations

iii)   superficial plots
iv)   obscured (camouflaged) social criticism

All of these would form the foundation of a basic model for the Hollywood family melodrama.

However, it is important to note that Schatz's discussion culminated in the establishment of Douglas Sirk as not only a 'complex genius' but also as the archetypal melodramatist. Curiously, this was in spite of the fact that at one point Schatz noted that Sirk was '[in] style and attitude fundamentally at odds with many, if not most, of the other melodramatists' (1981: 246). Schatz described how Sirk developed a unique approach to the creation of the Hollywood family melodrama in the 1950s. Whilst many of the key themes and character-types of melodrama were retained, Sirk handled these in more ambivalent and detached ways than his colleagues. For instance, Sirk orchestrated audience sympathies and emotions in significantly different ways from most other melodramatists (and from most other Hollywood directors): namely, by refusing to adopt the happy-ending more typical of Hollywood melodramas in general. Despite recognising (even celebrating) Sirk's difference and unconventionality, Schatz took the director not just as a special case but also as the most profound exponent of the Hollywood family melodrama. His extensive analysis of Sirk's films (namely, *All That Heaven Allows, Written on the Wind* and *Imitation of Life*) provided a vivid picture of the Hollywood family melodrama. What made these particular films so striking was that they not only employed some of the basic themes identified in other films (such as *Picnic, Giant* and *Peyton Place*) but exaggerated them. The style and thematic content of Sirk's films came to dominate Schatz's chapter on the family melodrama, making it seem that these films (and this approach) was what melodrama was really all about. This was in spite of the fact, of course, that these very films were simultaneously presented as an alternative to standard Hollywood melodrama.

If, in the early 1980s, Thomas Schatz's work provided the clearest sense of what a basic model of the Hollywood family melodrama consisted of, this was largely a consolidation of work carried out by film scholars in the 1970s. It was also an affirmation of some basic assumptions and critical perspectives. Douglas Sirk and his 1950s' films were assigned a privileged role in this process of defining the family melodrama as a genre and making that genre stand in for melodrama as a whole. Consequently, Film Studies came to adopt a model of melodrama that, in many crucial

11

ways, was actually set apart from other forms of popular film melodrama. It is important to remember that this model was determined by a specific set of interests, for example ideology, psychoanalysis and feminism. It is just as important to recognise that these interests influenced the way its key directors and films were adopted as representative of the genre as a whole. Had another set of interests prevailed at this time, different film-makers and a different group of films would have been privileged, constituting a different model. However, let us now consider how these concerns impacted on the model of the family melodrama.

A basic model

First and foremost, the basic model chiefly concerns the conflicts and tensions of a middle-class family. More often than not, this conflict is between the generations. In general, the drama is set within an affluent or upwardly-mobile situation and, whilst social and economic concerns are often present, the emphasis tends to be on personal emotional traumas. For instance, in *Giant*, Jett Rink (James Dean) is so consumed with envy of the film's central protagonist, Jordan Benedict (Rock Hudson), that he seeks to possess all he owns, his cattle ranch, wife (Elizabeth Taylor) and daughter. Striking oil on his small plot of land transforms Jett into a wealthy and powerful tycoon capable of buying the Benedict ranch (that is, their home and livelihood) and seducing the youngest daughter. Ultimately though, both of these elude him and despite his success he becomes a tragic and ridiculous figure, alcoholic and consumed with self-pity. Benedict meanwhile is able to preserve his home and family. Interwoven with this story, however, is a persistent criticism of capitalism (particularly the corporate oil industry) and racial prejudice. The Benedict family at the heart of the film struggle to survive and maintain their unity in the face of these two particular threats as well as those of Jett Rink; Rink simultaneously being the embodiment of capitalism and racial bigotry. The challenge they face is to maintain their affection and respect for each other when confronted by these economic and social forces as well as the individualised one (in the character of Rink).

The model of the Hollywood family melodrama is also characterised by its central protagonist, who tends to be privileged by a high degree of audience identification. In this way, the audience is invited (or, indeed, induced) to sublimate their own fears and anxieties onto the central figure who is, in most cases, also the victim of the drama. This figure could either be the son, daughter or the mother but almost never a father. In fact, it is the father who tends to remain throughout these films the most unsympathetic figure, even more so when absent or deceased. Classic examples of dominating fathers reducing their sons to tortured victims can be found in such films as *East of Eden*, where the father is played by Raymond Massey, and *Cat on a Hot Tin Roof*, featuring Big Daddy (Burl Ives).

Frequently, in family melodramas, the emphasis is on the direct portrayal of the psychological situation, which the audience is likely to share and understand from their own experiences of family life. Elements of Freudian repression are often depicted as symptoms such as hysteria, oedipal conflict, impotence and alcoholism (see Elsaesser 1972). The 'Return of the Repressed' has, in fact, been noted to emerge within the film-text itself, in the form of a discontinuity in the narrative (see Nowell-Smith 1977). At certain moments, a breaking-down of 'reality' appears, which can be understood as the hysterical moment of the text. At this point, the *mise-en-scène* has a tendency to become explicitly symbolic or coded, with the added accompaniment of heavily repetitive and intrusive music. A classic example of this is when, in *Rebel Without a Cause*, Jim Stark (James Dean) destroys a painted portrait of his mother, by kicking it, tearing through the canvas. This action comes immediately after physically attacking his father and being pulled off by his mother. The action of damaging his mother's portrait as he storms out of the house appears to symbolise his desire to hit or even kill her. Moreover, breaking through the fabric of the painting simultaneously breaks the 'reality' of the scene when (or if) the audience notices how convenient it was that this portrait just happened to be (strategically placed) on the floor against the door, barring his exit from the home that he finds so stultifying. The logic of the painting being there at this crucial moment and thereby enabling the symbolic act of filial aggression has the potential to reveal the contrivance of the scene (and the placement of this prop) which simultaneously ruptures the realism of the film itself. The use of spectacle, dramatic action and suspense are especially important in any melodrama, the action being worked up toward bold and effective climaxes, with strong local effects, such as this scene from *Rebel Without a Cause*. Music is used to mark the emotional events, constituting a system of punctuation, heightening the expressive and emotional contrasts of the storyline. In such moments, music makes these films much more dramatic and, by the same token, less like real life.

A further characteristic feature of the family melodrama, is that of wish-fulfilment and the tendency to culminate the drama in a happy ending.

However, there are many cases when such an ending appears, realistically, to be impossible or at least highly improbable. Nevertheless, a happy-ending in the conventional narrative film appears to be almost compulsory and this means that in melodrama artistic license has frequently to be taken (see the examples in the next section for instances of this). In cases where a satisfactory narrative resolution proves to be impossible, the erup-tion of excesses in the film-text prove to be impossible to contain, render-ing any closure forced and, moreover, exposing ideological contradictions at this point. As Geoffrey Nowell-Smith argued in his formative essay on melodrama in the late 1970s,

> ... the importance of melodrama lies precisely in its ideological fail-ure. Because it cannot accommodate its problems either in a real present or an ideal future, but lays them open in their contradictori-ness, it opens a space which most Hollywood films have studiously closed off. (1977: 118)

Case studies: Broken Blossoms, Stella Dallas and Rebel Without a Cause

This basic model has proved to be highly flexible, enabling very different kinds of film to be discussed in relation to each other – as melodrama. So, for instance, if we take three very different films from three distinct periods of Hollywood film history, we can see how, despite obvious differences, they appear to conform closely to the model in all its key aspects (as outlined above). Take the following examples: *Broken Blos-soms* (1919), *Stella Dallas* (1937) and *Rebel Without a Cause* (1955). All three films have at various times been studied and analysed in detail as examples of melodrama by leading critics, theorists and historians of film. All three though are very different. They employ quite different styles of acting, for instance. They use noticeably different styles of cinematog-raphy – black and white in the case of *Broken Blossoms* and *Stella Dallas*, colour and widescreen in the case of *Rebel Without a Cause*. They have different thematic concerns at the heart of their narratives – race and miscegenation in *Broken Blossoms*, class in *Stella Dallas* and teenage angst and non-conformity in *Rebel Without a Cause*. Yet the basic model of the Hollywood family melodrama enables these very different films to be understood (and studied) in relation to each other. Certain key fea-tures linking these films emerge when they are simultaneously compared to the basic model. [3]

Firstly, all three films depict conflicts and tensions within the family, particularly conflicts between the generations. *Broken Blossoms* depicts a dysfunctional working-class family in the Limehouse district of London in the late 1800s. 'Battling Burrows' (Donald Crisp) is an uncouth prize-fighter who mercilessly beats his frail motherless daughter Lucy (Lilian Gish). Lucy's only salvation is the gentle kindness of a sensitive and holy (Buddhist) Chinese store-keeper, Cheng Huan (Richard Barthelmess). *Stella Dallas* depicts an equally fragmented family. Here the daughter Laurel (Anne Shirley) is torn between her estranged parents, the lower-class Stella (Barbara Stanwyck) and the upper-class Stephen (John Boles), her future happiness and marital prospects being entirely dependent upon which parent she chooses to live with. To enable Laurel to make the 'right' decision (that is, one that is the most socially acceptable and advantageous), Stella is ultimately forced to turn her beloved daughter against her, forsaking her devotion. In *Rebel Without a Cause*, gender roles are at the heart of the Stark family's domestic tensions. The son, Jim (James Dean) is driven towards adolescent delinquency due to his domineering mother (Ann Doren) and his feminised father (Jim Backus).

All three films place a victim hero/ine at the centre of the narrative and afford them privileged audience identification and knowledge. Lucy (the daughter) is the tragic victim of *Broken Blossoms*, a victim of poverty and domestic brutality. Not only is she brutalised by her father, she has been brought up without the love and affection of her mother, in abject poverty and a bleak and hostile environment, so surrounded by ugliness and despair that she has never had cause to smile. Consequently, the only way to put a smile on her face, when commanded by her father, is to force the corners of her mouth upwards with her fingers. Witnessing Lucy's repeated beatings, the audience is shown that this harsh treatment is unwarranted and unjust, her meek compliance and inability to rebel or escape provoking extreme audience sympathy. Stella (the mother) is the victim of the film that bears her married name, *Stella Dallas*. Married above her station, Stella's dreams of upward mobility turn into a nightmare when she proves an unsuitable companion for her upper-class husband and an unsuitable mother for her middle-class daughter. Her daughter's friends and associates ridicule her for her lack of taste and decorum, repeatedly snubbing Laurel once they learn the identity of her mother. To enable Laurel to enjoy the lifestyle and social status that she herself once dreamed of, Stella realises she must turn her daughter away from her and allow her father to help her make her way in life: that is, marry into middle-class respectability. Stella is forced to sacrifice the one thing in life she has come to love above all things, her daughter. In *Rebel Without a Cause*, Jim (the son) is the victim of his own frustrations, in the grip of a teenage crisis. Having a weak father, he lacks an appropriate male role model to live up to, until his delinquency (drunkeness, car chases, knife-fights, and so on) brings him into contact with Ray Framek (Edward Platt), a police officer in the Juvenile Division. Framek's influence stabilises Jim and enables him to become a man, as does his burgeoning relationship with Judy (Natalie Wood). In the process, Jim forgoes his criminal activities and his association with social outsiders and misfits, including the troubled and sensitive – implicitly homosexual – Plato (Sal Mineo).

A key feature of all three films is the way the action is worked up to bold climaxes, music marking the emotional events, and swinging suddenly from one emotion to its extreme opposite. In *Broken Blossoms*, for instance, the film begins in a place of innocence, a happy sunlit haven populated by happy smiling people. This is a Chinese port, where we are first introduced to Cheng Huan. From here we shift to the dark and drab setting of London's Limehouse district, misty and mysterious, threatening and ugly. Here people look miserable, exhausted and suspicious. We first meet Lucy in this environment, wandering about the docks, encountering exhausted housewives and cynical prostitutes. Her home though is no refuge. Upon entering it she is threatened by her father. Although on this occasion she is spared a whipping, he taunts and humiliates her, forcing her to smile (with fear and tears in her eyes). This scene is full of tension due to the threat of violence. It is followed by a period of calm as Lucy sits alone at home and then goes out to the shops. She returns, however, to find her father in a rage and intent on venting his frustration on her. The scene culminates in her being beaten. A quieter passage follows in which Lucy makes her unsteady way back to the shops, staggering into Cheng Huan's shop and fainting on the floor. Scenes of great tenderness and gentleness follow, as he cares for her but these represent the calm before the great storm, in which Lucy is beaten to death by her father. Similarly, *Stella Dallas* juxtaposes moments of calm and happiness with moments of hysteria and tears. A notable instance here is when Laurel comes home from school and discovers a new party dress that her mother has been making. The squeals of delight turn swiftly to tears when Stella is angry that her planned surprise has been discovered too soon. Order and happiness though are quickly restored when Stella allows Laurel to try the garment on but Laurel is soon in tears again when her mother's gentle-

FIGURE 1 Cheng Huan confronts Battling Burrows in *Broken Blossoms*

man friend discovers her taking off the dress and teases her. Similarly, Laurel's ecstatic response to the sight of her birthday table and cake dissolves into sad resignation when none of her invited guests turn up for the party. A prominent feature of the film is that Laurel's moments of jubilation turn instantly into sadness and tears, moments of joy always followed by moments of despair.

Psychological and Freudian overtones are evident in all three films. This takes the form of the father's implicit rape of his daughter in *Broken Blossoms*, smashing through the door of a closet with an axe, dragging Lucy out and beating her to death on his bed. A key feature of this act is the phallic imagery, namely the axe and the whip. In *Stella Dallas* the Freudian connection is the initial strong attachment between mother and daughter that is traumatically broken in favour of the relationship between daughter and father, enabling the daughter to mature into adulthood. *Rebel Without a Cause*, on the other hand, is filled with images of sublimated passion, displaced aggression, sexual and gender ambiguity and impotence (such as when Jim's father is depicted wearing a frilly apron, crawling on the floor having dropped his wife's breakfast tray).

Finally, all three films have ambiguous (and somewhat unsatisfactory) endings. *Broken Blossoms* ends with the father getting his 'just dessert.'

FIGURE 2   Stella and her beloved Laurel in *Stella Dallas*

There is something deeply satisfying about the moment when the loutish bully is shot dead by Cheng Huan. Nevertheless, the hero and heroine also die in the process, in the tradition of doomed, star-crossed lovers. The death of the evil father is small consolation for the death of these two, whose tentative expressions of love are cut off in their prime. *Stella Dallas* ends with the heartrending maternal sacrifice of Stella watching her beloved daughter being married into middle-class respectability, watching through a window, outside in the rain, clinging to the railings and all too quickly moved on by a policeman. This devastating scenario, however, is followed by Stella's final moments in the film as she strides triumphantly towards the camera, smiling through her tears, achievement writ large across her worn-out face. Meanwhile, at the end of *Rebel Without a Cause*, Jim (James Dean) is reconciled with his family (particularly his father) having forsaken his rebellious ways in favour of family life, not only as a dutiful son to his parents but also as the prospective husband of Judy (Natalie Wood). His red jacket – the symbol of his rebellious status throughout the movie – has been handed over to Plato who has been, in the climactic scene, shot by the police. Though this represents a restoration of the status quo, the loss of the sensitive and troubled outsider Plato and the banal conservatism of Jim's new-found conformity represent two forms of critical loss at the end of this movie. None of these films, in other words, achieves a satisfactory happy ending nor brings the goals and ambitions of the characters to fruition. Lucy does not gain the tender devotion she craved in contrast to her brutal and impoverished upbringing. Stella does not achieve her dream of social respectability and status nor even recognition as a good mother. Jim does not achieve an alternative lifestyle to the stifling suburban conventionality of his parents. In all cases, the viewer is allowed to understand these motivations and identify with them, only to see them thwarted. The problems posed by the films have not therefore found a satisfactory solution. This suggests that for the characters at the heart of these films, the social order can offer no satisfactory solution to their problems, their desires being impossible to accommodate fully within the existing social system.

FIGURE 3 The aftermath of the chicken-run in *Rebel Without a Cause*

Reading against the grain

For film scholars interested in examining the ideology of Hollywood cinema, melodrama and the specific genre of the 'family melodrama' offered a striking instance where the filmic system could be seen to buckle under the weight of ideological contradiction, exposing the failings of capitalism and/or patriarchy. Neo-Marxist and feminist film scholars were drawn to this debate in the late 1970s. Underlying the whole debate on melodrama in the 1970s was the notion of ideology as defined by the Neo-Marxist philosopher Louis Althusser. From an Althusserian standpoint, every sphere of life is determined one way or another by ideology, from politics and religion to ambitions, desires and manners. More specifically, ideology arises in association with processes of communication and exchange. Fundamentally, it is a means by which the existing arrangement of social relations represents itself to individuals. In other words, it is the image a society gives itself in order to perpetuate itself and maintain the status quo. Such representations therefore serve to constrain and establish fixed positions for individuals in society, using the fabrication of images and the processes of representation to persuade us that how things are is how they ought to be. It is the construction therefore of such notions as the 'natural' and the 'normal', constructed according to the 'dominant' ideology that prevails across broad sections of society and, most especially, within what is known as the 'establishment' (state institutions, religious authorities, the mainstream media, and so on).

According to these arguments, dominant ideology is specific to a particular culture at a particular moment of its history. Moreover, it can be distinguished from particular ideologies (alternative, subversive, subcultural and marginal ideologies) which relate more closely to the lived experience of groups and classes, with specific and separate identities, values, ideas, customs, etc. As American society, like all advanced western capitalist societies, is characterised by divisions of class, gender, race, sex and ethnicity, the purpose of the dominant ideology is to establish and maintain a consensus, valid for all members of society. The operations of the dominant ideology are therefore a ceaseless effort to mask or displace both its own contradictions and those that have arisen from alternative ideologies: for example, the contradiction within dominant ideology between its championing of equality and its necessary commitment to inequality.

What emerged from the initial study of Hollywood melodrama as a genre (that is, the Hollywood family melodrama) was that it was not only fascinating and highly entertaining in its own right but, moreover, that it was an appropriate and valuable register of ideology and ideological contradiction. In particular, melodrama's very failure, its many moments of excess which provoke disbelief, irony, laughter and a whole host of other unwelcome emotions from its audience, became the Neo-Marxist film historian's gain. It was precisely this aspect of melodrama that made it so appropriate a subject of study for the historian seeking to prise the gaps and cracks open further to reveal the world behind the scenes. And indeed, behind each of the films analysed by Elsaesser or Nowell-Smith, there appeared to be a society and a particular set of cultural values and beliefs.

Elsaesser's article, 'Tales of Sound and Fury' (1972), was the first notable study of melodrama, representing many of the concerns and preoccupations of critical thinking of the 1970s. In this article, Elsaesser suggested that, under certain social and production conditions, melodrama could be seen as ideologically subversive. For Elsaesser, the family is not just an important political institution in itself but is also a means through which social crises can be delineated in personalised and emotional terms. He noted the emergence in the 1950s of the impotent hero, trapped within a domestic interior and confined by codes of behaviour appropriate to the family. This he took as an indication of the shift in the ideological conditions pertaining under post-war advanced capitalism. Moreover, for Elsaesser, this represented a shift to a critique of individualism, in which the bourgeois family became the site of both social and emotional isolation and, consequently, of the failure of the drive to self-fulfilment.[4]

Reading excess as ideological contradiction

Geoffrey Nowell-Smith continued the ideological debate on melodrama in 1977 in his essay 'Minnelli and Melodrama'. Here he drew on Freudian psychoanalysis to account for the excessive style of Hollywood melodrama, and his essay is based on an analysis of the films of Vincente Minnelli. Though perhaps best known for his popular musicals, such as *Meet Me in St Louis* (1944) (starring his wife, Judy Garland) and *An American in Paris* (1951), Minnelli also directed a succession of melodramas. *The Bad and the Beautiful* (1952), starring Kirk Douglas as a Hollywood producer, concerns the cut-throat world of the film industry and its ambitious denizens and deals with similar themes to both Billy Wilder's *Sunset Boulevard* (1950) and Joseph L. Manciewicz's *All About Eve* (1950). *The Cobweb* (1955) is a male melodrama concerning the troubled relationship between the proprietor of a psychiatric clinic and his sexually demanding wife and mistress. *Home From the Hill* (1959) is a Texan family melodrama, in the manner of Douglas Sirk's *Written on the Wind*. *Some Came Running* (1958) is another male melodrama, dealing with a writer returning to his hometown following the Second World War. Perhaps most controversially *Tea and Sympathy* (1956) tells the story of a teacher's wife who attempts to 'convert' a 17-year-old student who demonstrates the signs of latent homosexuality (expressed, primarily, as a lack of interest in sport).

Though Nowell-Smith's essay confines itself to observations based on two of Minnelli's musicals (*The Pirate* and *Meet Me in St Louis*) and *The Cobweb*, many of Minnelli's melodramas, as well as those made by Nicholas Ray and Douglas Sirk, reveal the latent repression that is the focus of his analysis. Nowell-Smith's essay is concerned with the Freudian concept of conversion hysteria, which enables him to construct a symptomatic reading of the cinema of the 1950s. Nowell-Smith notes that Freud observed that patients undergoing psychoanalysis could be identified as repressing strong emotions, which have been pushed into the unconscious. These repressed emotions often then emerge, in a perverse way, as physical symptoms, a condition usually described as conversion hysteria or as 'the return of the repressed'. Nowell-Smith suggests that there is a clear parallel between the process of conversion hysteria and the excessive style (and excessive behaviours) evident in the Hollywood melodramas of the 1950s and Minnelli's films in particular.

He first points out that we should recognise that melodramas are not stories concerned with action and an active protagonist but rather they are principally concerned with emotion. Broadly speaking, in the American movie the active hero becomes the protagonist of the western, the passive or impotent hero or heroine becomes the protagonist of what has come to be known as the melodrama (Gledhill 1987: 72). Nowell-Smith believes that this means that melodrama's characters are noted by their inability to take action to resolve their problems; they are effectively oppressed and repressed individuals. He suggests that, as a consequence of this passivity and inaction, we see emotions and tensions building up that cannot be turned into action and then resolved in a satisfactory fashion. It is certainly true to say that films from this period seem to be bursting with pent-up emotion, with things characters cannot say or do and information that the narrative cannot reveal or depict. Because of this, Nowell-Smith suggests that repressed emotions erupt in moments of high tension or drama and manifest themselves as symptoms through performance, music and *mise-en-*

scène and it is at such points of heightened emotion that the characteristic excesses of the melodrama manifest themselves. In Nowell-Smith's words:

> The laying out of the problems 'realistically' always allows for the generating of an excess which cannot be accommodated. The more the plots press towards a resolution the harder it is to accommodate the excess. What is characteristic of the melodrama, both in its original sense and in the modern one, is the way the excess is siphoned off. The undischarged emotion which cannot be accommodated within the action, subordinated as it is to the demands of family/lineage/inheritance, is traditionally expressed in the music and in the case of film, in certain elements of the *mise-en-scène*. That is to say, music and *mise-en-scène* do not heighten the emotionality of an element of the action: to some extent they substitute for it. (1987: 73)

Here Nowell-Smith argues that at points of high drama the melodrama that usually aims to convey a strong sense of realism (for example, by using the rhetorical conventions of Classical Hollywood cinema) literally exceeds the limits of what can be considered realistic; it goes 'over the top'. Nowell-Smith is suggesting that there is such an excess of conflict and contradiction that the narrative cannot contain it and that, consequently, realism and narrative coherence breaks down. Like a saucepan full to the lid with boiling water, the excess emotion leaks out. It is at such highly emotional points that hysterical conversion takes place, that the repressed starts to emerge. At such points, the *mise-en-scène* directly represents the emotions and conflicts that the film's narrative and characters cannot articulate (for example, the damaged portrait of Jim Stark's mother in *Rebel Without a Cause*).

This account provides an explanation of the expressionistic and extravagant *mise-en-scène* that Minnelli and many of his contemporary directors used: most notably Douglas Sirk and Nicholas Ray. This psychoanalytic model proved to be an extremely useful way of understanding the excessive moments in Sirk's films, generally accepted as being the most excessive of all the 1950s Hollywood melodramatists. Marylee's (Dorothy Malone) so-called 'dance of death' in *Written on the Wind* provides an excellent example. In the scene, Marylee is escorted home to the Hadley residence by the police, after an evening's debauchery. At the same time, her father, Jasper Hadley, is presented with the shocking revelation that his daughter is a 'tramp' by the service station attendant that she has been found with. Marylee returns to her bedroom and starts to play 'Temptation' on a record player changing from her evening dress into a lurid pink negligée. As Jasper Hadley climbs the sweeping staircase to confront his daughter the tempo and volume of the music increases and, through an increasingly frantic montage of parallel edits, the audience sees Marylee and her father simultaneously. Whilst Marylee dances ever more frenetically, almost at the top of the stairs, with the music blaring, Jasper has a heart attack and falls back down the stairs at the same time as Marylee falls into a seat waving her legs in the air. Marylee's sexual energy (and implied nymphomania) was a subject that a 1950s film could not possibly depict naturalistically. It is therefore transformed in this extraordinarily hysterical scene, into a frantic dance that not only disrupts family harmony and causes the death of her father but also creates an excess that disrupts the conventions of cinematic realism.

For Nowell-Smith 'excess' acts as a safety valve, siphoning off the ideological contradictions that cannot be resolved in the narrative of the melodrama. Laura Mulvey also used this idea in her essay 'Notes on Sirk and Melodrama' in which she argues that it is in fact a feminine point of view represented in the Hollywood melodrama that results in the excessive style of these films. Mulvey points out that there is a fundamental difference, at a narrative and discursive level, between the male melodrama and the female point of view melodrama. The former, such as Minnelli's *The Cobweb* or *Home From the Hill*, although excessive, arrives ultimately at some kind of final satisfactory conclusion. By contrast, the melodramas with a female point of view, such as *All That Heaven Allows*, tend to deny a satisfactory conclusion and often end in a very contradictory fashion.

> It is as though having a female point of view dominating the narrative produces an excess which precludes satisfaction. If the melodrama offers a fantasy escape for the identifying women in the audience, the illusion is so strongly marked by recognisable, real and familiar traps that the escape is closer to a daydream than a fairytale. (Mulvey 1987: 82)

A feminist critique of film melodrama

From 1977 onwards, when Film Studies adopted melodrama and Hollywood's films for women as major areas for research and debate, film scholars repeatedly demonstrated the extent to which patriarchal ideology was deeply embedded within these movies. Laura Mulvey and Chuck Kleinhans initiated a line of critical enquiry into melodrama that would largely determine the agenda for many years, one that would be developed and refined in the work of Barbara Creed, Christine Gledhill, Mary Ann Doane, Lea Jacobs and Tania Modleski.

In his 1978 essay 'Notes on Melodrama and the Family Under Capitalism', Chuck Kleinhans described the family as a political institution and as a site of real oppression, for women especially. He pointed out that the nature of the family allows it to function in society as a trans-class institution that reproduces individuals as both class and sexed subjects. Taking a Marxist-feminist sociological approach, Kleinhans characterised the social relations of capitalist production in terms of a split between 'productive' work and personal life confined to the home, in effect the 'sphere of reproduction'. In this way, women and children are marginalised outside of production. He argued that one of the most fundamental contradictions of capitalist society is the notion that people's problems can be solved in their private life. Women, as the guardians of the home, are effectively required to provide the rewards and satisfactions that have otherwise proved unobtainable in public life. Kleinhans recognised that family melodramas employed the same process of displacement by making the family and the domestic context the arena for articulating social pressures and problems, frustrations and dissatisfaction. In so doing, the burden of solving social problems is placed largely with the female characters. In most instances, the female characters in family melodramas attempt to solve these problems and maintain the family (that is, to resolve familial conflict) through the repression of their own desires and other acts of self-sacrifice.

Writing around the same time as Kleinhans, Barbara Creed pursued a feminist investigation into the patriarchal ideology of melodrama in her essay 'The Position of Women in Hollywood Melodramas', as did Laura Mulvey. All three publications had in fact emerged out of the same context, a weekend school organised in London (25–27 March 1977) by the Society for Education in Film and Television (SEFT), an event which feminist scholar Griselda Pollock reported on in *Screen* later that year. It is clear from Pollock's report that this event had a decidedly feminist agenda and, with hindsight, it can be seen to have marked the beginning of the second stage of scholarship on melodrama. This represented a shift in two important directions. Firstly, a shift from male film scholars interested in questions of *mise-en-scène*, genre and ideology to feminist scholars interested in Hollywood's attempts to cater for female audiences. Secondly, a shift from recognising melodrama's potential progressiveness or subversiveness to revealing its more conservative and repressive aspects. Mulvey's essay played a seminal role here. Noted for her groundbreaking feminist critique of Hollywood cinema, 'Visual Pleasure and Narrative Cinema', Mulvey turned her attention towards Hollywood's films for women and, in particular, its female-centred melodramas (mainly directed by Douglas Sirk). Her essay on melodrama was initially presented at the SEFT weekend school in March 1977, published in the Winter edition (1977/78) of the journal *Movie* and subsequently reprinted in Christine Gledhill's *Home is Where the Heart Is* (1987). In part, the importance of this essay was that it established the notion of melodrama as a 'safety valve' for enacting the contradictions of family and sexual relations under patriarchy. Here melodrama was regarded as a means for the patriarchal order to sustain itself through a temporary and fictionalised acknowledgement of its repressive effects upon half the population (that is, women). However, her essay was also important for initiating what was to become the new and dominant line of enquiry into Hollywood's films for women. Mulvey made a critical distinction between two types of melodrama: one dominated by a female protagonist's viewpoint, another that deals with the oedipal problems of a male hero (as fellow victim of patriarchal society). The latter referred to the genre as it had been established and described by Elsaesser and Nowell-Smith. The former was prompted by the films of Douglas Sirk that centred on female characters (namely, *All That Heaven Allows* and *Imitation of Life*) but, potentially, it referred to a much larger and long-standing category of films made for a female audience: for instance, 'women's weepies', romantic and costume dramas. This much more diverse category of cinema subsequently became the basis of Mary Ann Doane's research during the 1980s. It also provided the basis for many future discussions of 'melodrama and the Woman's Film,' for instance, in the work of Christine Gledhill in the 1980s.

Melodrama and the woman's film find a home together

Christine Gledhill produced an important chapter on melodrama for *The Cinema Book* (Cook 1984) in which she assessed and explained the published literature on film melodrama from 1971 to 1983. This represented the first major summing up of the debate on melodrama within Film Studies, describing and to some extent evaluating the writing of

Elsaesser, Nowell-Smith, Kleinhans, Mulvey and Creed, and introducing the 'new feminism' of Lea Jacobs, Mary Ann Doane and Tania Modleski. Gledhill's feminist agenda in reviewing and summing up the melodrama debate within Film Studies is clear from her criticisms of Elsaesser's seminal study of the genre. She criticised him for failing to investigate how a female protagonist affects plot structures and for not attempting to distinguish the family melodrama from women's films and romantic drama. In contrast, the emergence of a feminist project on melodrama was described in more positive terms, with a general conclusion that the major interest of melodrama for feminist film scholars lay chiefly in revealing the ironies and instabilities of Hollywood's attempts to reproduce the contradictions of femininity under patriarchy.

A number of the essays reviewed by Gledhill in *The Cinema Book* would, a few years later, form the basis of her edited collection of studies on melodrama and the woman's film, *Home is Where the Heart Is* (1987). The essays of Elsaesser, Nowell-Smith and Mulvey were reprinted alongside works by a second generation of scholars. It is clear that by 1987 feminist scholarship had come to dominate research on film melodrama, hence twelve of the total nineteen essays included in this collection were feminist investigations (or critiques). Moreover, nine of these were concerned with the 'woman's film'. Both Gledhill's chapter on melodrama in *The Cinema Book* and her subsequent anthology indicate that within Film Studies 'melodrama' and the 'woman's film' had became largely synonymous during the 1980s. It is important to remember, however, that the films discussed by Elsaesser in his 1972 study of the Hollywood family melodrama were not made for exclusively female audiences and could not be described as women's films. Indeed, for him, their significance was primarily for male audiences. Mulvey's 1977/78 essay had, of course, recognised this but it had also recognised what was missing: films for women. Subsequently, the feminist project within Film Studies (largely inspired by Mulvey's intervention) was to redress this imbalance. So successful was it that, for a time at least, feminist film scholars led the debate on melodrama: that debate being, very largely, a debate about Hollywood's (and Gainsborough's) films for women. However, in the 1990s the debate shifted again. By this time, feminist interest had moved either towards television (for example, soap opera) or to films and videos made by women for women. It was at this point, that a critical new intervention into understanding melodrama as genre was made by two leading genre theorists, Steve Neale and Rick Altman.

Redefining the Film Studies' account of melodrama

In 1993, Steve Neale's article 'Melo Talk: On the Meaning and Use of the Term "Melodrama" in the American Trade Press' attempted a radical revision of the Film Studies' conception of melodrama. Revealing that the term 'melodrama' was used originally in Hollywood to designate films featuring crime, guns and violence, along with action, tension and suspense, Neale showed how radically at odds the Film Studies' notion of melodrama was compared to that of the film industry that created these movies. Whilst for film scholars in the 1970s and 1980s, 'melodrama' was taken to mean female-oriented weepies and male oedipal dramas set within the context of the family, for the film reviewers and critics in the 1940s and 1950s 'melodrama' meant male-oriented thrillers, chillers and action movies.

Neale subsequently reworked his essay as a chapter on melodrama and the woman's film in his book *Genre and Hollywood* (2000). Here he noted that, within Film Studies, since the mid-1970s, a number of things had been attributed to cinematic melodrama: an antecedence, an aesthetic, a critical status, a generic (or sub-generic) categorisation, and even a gender-specific audience. All of these, he argued, were questionable. In fact, he held Thomas Elsaesser and Douglas Sirk equally responsible for the genesis of the 'standard account' of melodrama: Elsaesser through his highly influential 1972 essay and Sirk through his published interview with Jon Halliday in *Sirk on Sirk* (1971). Both film scholar and director had been instrumental in the establishment of a canon of films understood as 'melodrama', along with a basic set of terms, concerns and definitions, and a topic of investigation, discussion and debate: in other words, they set the agenda. Neale was concerned to establish a precise historical account of 'melodrama'; in contrast to the 1970s and 1980s engagement with neo-Marxism, film scholarship in the 1990s was characterised by a return to historicism and something of a backlash against 'Theory' with a capital T. This period also saw the emergence of 'reception studies' with Film Studies, in which investigations were conducted into the ways that actual audiences (that is, specific social groups) interpreted a specific group of films or an individual film in a particular place and time. Reception studies of cinema shifted the focus from theoretical analysis of film-texts to interviews with people about their earlier film-going experiences[5] or to extra-cinematic material in circulation at the time of a film's release – press ads, reviews, publicity, journalistic articles, and so on.[6]

Neale's approach to investigating melodrama can be seen as part of a larger project in Film Studies in the 1990s to re-evaluate established accounts of film history from the new perspective of reception studies. In revising the 1970s and 1980s Film Studies' account of melodrama, Neale would challenge virtually every major aspect of it: disputing the relevance of the 'family melodrama' as the ultimate form, dissociating melodrama from the 'woman's film' and proposing an alternative basic model. All of this was achieved, of course, by his adoption of an entirely different method of investigation from the earlier generations of melodrama scholars. His alternative conception of 'melodrama' was based on definitions and designations of the term in film review journalism in a selection of newspapers, film journals and the trade press. In short, he examined the way the terms 'melodrama', 'meller' and 'melodramatic' were used in film publications from the 1910s to the 1950s, in press releases and publicity sheets from the Hollywood studios. Amongst his most significant claims was that the term was not pejorative, implying low-status, and was not used to suggest an absence of realism. Nor did it imply a masculinity that was impaired, qualified, questioned or castrated (as assumed by Elsaesser, Mulvey and Nowell-Smith). Whilst noting the recurrence of terms such as 'vigorous melodrama', 'virile melodrama' and even 'he-man melodrama', Neale argued that terms such as 'romantic melodrama' or 'domestic melodrama' were rare and that the term 'family melodrama' was entirely absent.

Neale's investigation also revealed discrepancies between the American film industry's and the Film Studies' accounts of melodrama when he examined the discourses surrounding the 1950s canon – the films of Sirk, Ray, Ophüls and Minnelli. Here he found that the term 'melodrama' was used in reference to some of these films but not to describe their emotional or psychological aspects; rather to indicate their sensational themes. He notes, for instance, that Ray's *Rebel Without a Cause* was described as a melodrama by *Film Daily* due to its theme of juvenile delinquency, its knife fights and 'chickie-run' with stolen cars. Neale also noted that woman's films were rarely described as melodrama. Less than half the women's films made in Hollywood actually fit the standard account of melodrama, he argued, the greater proportion of woman's films being comedies, musicals, murder mysteries, historical dramas, westerns and gangster films.[7] Neale argued that from an industry perspective the women's films that were melodramas according to the industry's definition were the serial queen films: that is, sensational adventures built around a heroine, from the 1910s to early 1920s.[8] From his investigations into Hollywood's films for women, Neale insisted that the woman's film was anything but a despised and lowly genre, as many feminist film scholars in the 1970s and 1980s had claimed (for example, Molly Haskell, Mary Ann Doane and Christine Gledhill). On the contrary, Hollywood's films for women were, he claims, rather 'lofty', associated with 'taste' and 'quality' and aimed squarely at middle-class women.

Reconstructing melodrama's history

In tracing melodrama's antecedents and early development on screen, Steve Neale found that its recurrent features found their fullest expression not in the films defined as 'women's films' by 1980s feminist film scholars but rather in the big-production adventure and action movies. Neale spoke of a kinship between nineteenth-century melodrama and Hollywood's action and suspense genres. Melodrama's actions, he pointed out, involved bodies tied to rail-tracks, heroes in cellars with the water level rising, circular saws and steam hammers threatening the hero's life in some fiendish trap: all of which are more closely associated with the 'James Bond' film cycle than the films of Sirk and Minnelli.

Neale identified the key components of nineteenth-century stage melodrama as follows:

i)   conflict of good and evil
ii)   eventual triumph of good over evil
iii)   hero, heroine and villain as principal types
iv)   demonstrative and hyperbolic aesthetic
v)   episodic, formulaic and action-packed plots with fate, coincidence and chance playing a major role
vi)   'situations' (for example, tableaux) forming moments of dramatic revelation or display

Neale argued that such features are commonly found in the industry's conception of 'melodrama', where the term is used to describe gangster films, westerns, horror and war films. Meanwhile, such features are rarely found in Hollywood's romantic dramas, weepies and family dramas, which Film Studies has labelled 'melodrama'.

In the light of Neale's case against the Film Studies' account of melodrama, it has become a matter of concern that the conception of melodrama circulating in contemporary Film Studies is one that has emerged from within the discipline itself rather than the industry. Furthermore, this definition is at odds with the industry's own version, directly contradicting it. It may have proved to be a useful category for film scholars over the years, enabling them to designate a group of films that share a similar set of themes and stylistic features. It may also have enabled scholars to consider a specific group of films in relation to each other that otherwise belonged to very different production categories. For instance, understood as melodrama, *Now, Voyager*[9] (Irving Rapper, 1942) and *Written on the Wind*[10] can be compared in terms of their treatment of parental conflict, their use of Freudian psychoanalysis, and such issues as sexual repression or female independence. However, such a comparison may in fact distort the actual relationships between films that pertained for producers and audiences during the 1940s and 1950s. Given the growing importance of understanding films' historical reception, for many film scholars in the 1990s this may have been the deciding factor against the Film Studies' account of melodrama as a genre.

Steve Neale's intervention within the melodrama debate in the early 1990s led to a serious reassessment of this particular area of film scholarship. Highly polemical, it renewed discussion of melodrama within Film Studies, adding new impetus to a debate that had more or less fizzled out. It also, of course, stimulated vehement defence of the original Film Studies' account of melodrama, most notably from Rick Altman. Curiously, until this moment, Altman had expressed little interest in melodrama, concentrating his research into the Hollywood genre system on the musical (see his *Genre: The Musical* (1981) and *The American Film Musical* (1987)). However Altman was to provide the first chapter for *Refiguring American Genres* (Browne 1998). Here he not only proposed a new conception of Hollywood's genre system and the way genres evolve over time but also took melodrama and the woman's film as his primary focus. In so doing, Altman was able to directly contradict many of the claims previously made by Neale in his 'Melo Talk' essay of 1993.

In defence of the Film Studies account of melodrama

Rick Altman, in his earlier work on the musical, had offered an original thesis on the nature and effect of Hollywood's genre system. For instance, in the introduction to his book on the *American Film Musical*, he had argued that genre operates as a restrictive, even oppressive system to reduce the ability of audiences to read films freely (1987: 2). Consequently, part of the task of a critic or film scholar is to liberate films from the industry's generic categorisation of them (and the reading processes that this entails) enabling films to be opened up to freer interpretations. Altman's conception of the genre system was that it invariably links producers, their films and their audiences to an 'interpretative community' that produces meaning. This interpretative community is constituted chiefly by a specific set of 'intertexts', which are the other films that the industry identifies as belonging to the same genre. In consequence, this cuts out or delimits alternative ways for audiences to read, compare and draw meaning. This system, Altman argues, controls the audience's reaction to any specific film by providing the context in which that film is interpreted.

If we accept this situation, we need to consider whether the meanings constructed for a melodrama were governed or restricted by its relationship to another set of similar films. For instance, in its time was *Rebel Without a Cause* only considered (that is, interpreted) alongside other films dealing with juvenile delinquency (for example, *The Wild One*[11] (Stanley Kramer, 1954))? If so, did that obscure the significance of its father/son conflict that might have emerged more fully through comparison with, say, Richard Brooks' *Cat on a Hot Tin Roof*, where Paul Newman's character suffers from alcoholism and impotence as a result of his domineering father, Big Daddy? If the father/son conflict at the heart of these two films was the more critical social issue in the USA in the mid-to-late 1950s, then that would only emerge through the intervention of the Film Studies' account of melodrama that situates these two films within the same generic category. What the film industry had itself obscured through its different categorisation of these films would at last come to light in film scholarship, hence the value of the reclassification.

For Altman, 'genres are not the democratically elected representatives of a group of like-minded texts'. In fact he described them as 'autocratic monarchs dictating a single standard for all subjects' (1987: 5). The inference here is that by liberating films from the generic definitions once imposed on them by the (repressive) film industry, the film critic or historian can free their meanings, liberating a fuller regime of meaning. Consequently, for Altman, it is the task of critics and scholars to:

i)   explain the genre and its texts
ii) to create an appropriate vocabulary for the purposes of analysis
iii) to explain the function of a genre
iv) to establish its limits/boundaries (that is, its demarcation)

In the second part of his 1998 essay Altman refined his thinking on Hollywood's genre system as a direct result of Steve Neale's intervention in the melodrama debate, proposing a new model of generic process, one he calls 'genrification'. This investigation into how genres develop emerged, as had Neale's, from an examination of Hollywood publicity from the 1930s and 1940s. Altman noted that in press ads and posters for films of this period the generic specificity of the films were seldom mentioned and, more often, mixed generic categories was used to describe films. Film journalists, critics and reviewers, on the other hand, would more readily use generic terms to label individual films, as Neale has demonstrated. Altman revealed, however, that this latter group had very different objectives from the studio's publicity departments and therefore used generic terminology in very different ways. Moreover, he demonstrated that genres were always temporary classifications and thus what was designated 'melodrama' in the 1920s could well have changed radically by the 1950s. Altman noted that the lexicons of different ages are always retained and remain available, so that 'melodrama' in its original sense of thrills and spills could continue alongside newer notions of melodrama born out of 1970s film scholarship. Both uses of the term 'melodrama' remain available to studios, critics, journalists, audiences and scholars. Both therefore are relevant and valid, able to co-exist. In other words, the recognition of one does not invalidate the other.

Rick Altman argued that 'two generations of genre critics have done violence to the historical dimensions of genre [by] laying so much emphasis on generic fixity' (1998: 2). He also argued that recent genre theory has devoted too little attention to 'the logic and mechanisms whereby genres become recognisable as such' (ibid.). And this is precisely Altman's project; whilst traditional genre theory had highlighted coincident structures and concerns by ignoring difference and disagreement, Altman emphasised such discrepancies to reveal what makes difference within genres possible.

The genrification of melodrama and the woman's film

In the third and final part of his essay Rick Altman explores the confusions of genre definitions and demarcations in melodrama. It is here that he provides his most explicit counter-argument to that put forward by Steve Neale. First, Altman traces the antecedence of the term, locating the first use to 1770, by Rousseau in connection with his play 'Pygmalion'. Subsequently applied to many plays, novels and films, Altman notes that it has designated very different things and regards it as an 'evolving category'. He accuses some critics of holding on too tightly to generic terms, maintaining their consistency and continuity because they possess a level of prestige. He argues that it is primarily the critics that have a vested interest in reusing generic terms given that they make their subjective and historically specific readings appear universal and unchangeable. He notes that 'Whereas producers are actively destroying genres by creating new cycles ... critics are regularly trying to fold the cyclical differences into the genres, thus authorising continued use of a familiar, universalising, sanctioned, and therefore powerful term' (1998: 25). A clear instance of this, for Altman, is the project that emerged initially in the 1980s to draw attention to the inconsistent way in which the term 'melodrama' had been used, citing Russell Merritt's 'Melodrama: Postmortem for a Phantom Genre' (1983) and Ben Singer's 'Female Power in the Serial Queen Melodrama' (1990) as two early examples of this. However, Altman describes Steve Neale as 'the first scholar to directly tackle the disparity between recent and traditional definitions of film melodrama' (1998: 26).

Altman notes that in his bid to establish a fixed meaning for melodrama at odds with that in film scholarship, Neale has actually conflated the trades of film criticism/journalism with film production; that he has failed to recognise the disparities that Altman's own investigation has revealed. He suggests that Neale's main aim was to show that film scholars had misused the term 'melodrama' by applying it to woman's films and weepies. Altman's main concern here was to trace the history of the constitution of the woman's film as a genre and its connections with melodrama in order to come to terms with the problem of defining 'melodrama' posed by Neale. This is a highly instructive discussion that details the way in which the genre of the woman's film came about within Film Studies.

Altman starts with Molly Haskell's use of the term 'woman's film' in her book *From Reverence to Rape* in 1974. Here she used it to define a specific Hollywood genre and, significantly, repeatedly placed it within quotation marks as the 'woman's film'. Altman notes that Mary Ann Doane adopted the same practice in her first essays on Hollywood's films for women. Reminding us that the building of genres is usually a critical rather than production-based activity, he argues that Haskell and Doane created a genre by attaching the label 'woman's film' to a succession of different, already existing genres: in Doane's case, the woman's gothic, woman's horror, woman's film noir and woman's melodrama. Tellingly though, he points out that, in 1987, when Mary Ann Doane published her book *The*

Desire to Desire on Hollywood's films for women, based on the essays she had published in the early-to-mid-1980s, the quotation marks were dropped from the woman's film. This small but significant act, Altman suggests, marked the abandonment of 'any remnant of doubt regarding the category's right to independent existence' (1998: 31), although he does note some hestitation in Doane's conclusion to the first chapter. He interprets this as Doane hesitating about the generic status of the woman's film at the very point at which she is involved in changing that status, suggesting that, 'a major purpose of *The Desire to Desire* is to establish the woman's film as a genre' (ibid.). This process, Altman claims, involved 'the assimilation of the woman's film to an already established genre [melodrama] capable of lending to the woman's film some of its long-standing genericity' (ibid.). For this association to be effective, however, melodrama needed to be rethought as a genre addressed primarily to a female audience. Altman points out that

> Only when this junction took place ... would the woman's film abandon its quotation marks in favour of full generic status. Since the late 1980s, the generic status of the category has never been in doubt ... Indeed, a new generation of introductory texts has begun to treat the woman's film as fully the equal of established genres. (1998: 32)

This account helps us to understand why the categories of melodrama and the woman's film became synonymous in the 1980s, that this represented an important (even necessary) stage in the constitution of the 'woman's film' as a genre. Moreover, it also informs us of the need of a particular group of scholars to devise their own generic category. In this case, feminist film scholars, needing a coherent group of films that addressed issues of female subjectivity and desire, constructed a genre that the industry itself had avoided. Altman's account suggests that the film industry had little to gain economically from developing a genre of films for women, since it excluded a significant part of the cinema audience; that is, male viewers. An alternative, and more economically viable strategy, this argument would suggest, was to occasionally produce films for women within existing generic categories such as thrillers, horror movies, gangster pictures, historical costume dramas, and so on. Film critics, journalists and reviewers may have recognised these as films for women but the studios, according to Altman's thesis, would have been more likely to publicise these in general, stressing male and female appeal. In a sense, this could be thought of as a refusal on the part of the film studios to acknowledge that they were in fact producing a series of films built around female stars, with women as their central characters and appealing almost exclusively to female audiences. Feminist film scholars in the 1980s, however, had no such reason to deny this situation and, in fact, had some very good reasons for acknowledging that films for women (henceforth 'women's films') were a staple of Hollywood production throughout its history. Given that one of the primary objectives of feminist scholarship is the restoration of what has been hidden from history (that is, patriarchal histories), this was inevitably going to be one of the first tasks of feminist film scholarship.

Altman's examination of the construction of the family melodrama and the woman's film as genres in the 1970s and 1980s forms a major part of his project; a project that enabled him to formulate a new hypothesis for the genrification process. This consists of five main points:

i)   'The genre constitution process is not limited to a cycle's or genre's first appearance' (1998: 33)

ii)   'Taking one version of the genre as representative of the genre as a whole … is a normal step in the regenrification process' (1998: 34)

iii)   The prestige of a genre's label means that it is regularly retained for use for newly formed genres

iv)   'Any group of films may at any time be generically redefined by contemporary critics' (1998: 35)

v)   'critics recourse to regenrification as part of their critical and rhetorical arsenal is entirely expected, and in any case not preventable' (1998: 35–6)

Rick Altman's conception of genrification offers a useful way for us to retain the idea of melodrama as a genre. In particular, it allows the different forms of 'melodrama' in circulation at any one time – by film studios from the 1940s, film theorists from the 1970s and film historians from the 1990s – to co-exist. It enables us to understand why so many definitions of melodrama exist and circulate and allows us, as film scholars, to adopt any one (or several) of these where it is appropriate for our particular project.

Melodrama's on-going redefinition

The continued redefinition of melodrama, firstly in the 1970s by the film ideologists and, secondly, by feminist film scholars in the 1980s is, according to Altman's thesis, both an inevitable process of genrification and the very life-blood of the genre. In the absence of filmmakers continuing to produce the same, recognisable and established form of melodrama, film scholars have, in a sense, taken the lead in keeping melodrama alive as a genre by continually revising its corpus and its history. Moreover, film scholars have produced not only new understandings of the established generic model but also, more radically, they have reinvented the model itself. If this makes for a confusing account of a genre such as melodrama, it is only because of the persistence of a false assumption that genres exist as stable categories, used in the same way by film studios, publicists, journalists, critics and scholars alike and irrespective of time or history.

Melodrama owes its longevity to the fact that it has existed – and continues to exist – as a category of films defined differently at different times by different types of people (both within and beyond the film industry). Different kinds of film can be (have been and will continue to be) grouped together under this label not in any arbitrary fashion and not because anything can be thought of as melodrama but rather because it is an evolving form. It evolves with every new film that is made that refers directly to its established canon: such as *Far From Heaven* (Todd Haynes, 2002). It evolves with every advertisement that describes a film (old or new) as a melodrama or as melodramatic. It evolves when groups of film scholars discuss the meaning of the term and when a film historian discovers a print of an unknown film that can be said to manifest stylistic or thematic features redolent of what has previously been described as melodrama. It also evolves when new media forms refer to, are promoted as, or are otherwise described as having some resemblance or affinity to what is commonly held to be some existing form of melodrama. For some, however, this may seem too fluid, too slippery and too uncertain. For them, melodrama must either take one form or not be a genre at all. As melodrama has clearly never taken a single form and, over time, has developed many variants (that hardly seem to correspond at all in some cases), the alternative is to conceive of melodrama as something beyond genre. Numerous film scholars have adopted this approach since the 1980s. Melodrama has been re-articulated within Film Studies as several other things: a style, a mode and even a sensibility. In the remaining chapters of this book, we shall examine how melodrama has been thought of as something other than a genre and consider how appropriate and useful these approaches have proved to be.

2   STYLE

In chapter one we observed the debates and problems posed by the identification of melodrama as a distinct cinematic genre. The group of films
that we now categorise as melodrama have over time been identified vari-
ously as dramas, romantic dramas and perhaps most problematically as
'women's films'. We have seen that no fixed definition of what melodrama
means has emerged within Film Studies. The term is perhaps best understood as a critical category rather than a fixed unchanging cinematic genre.
As we have noted, this critical category emerged in the 1970s out of a specific set of academic interests: most notably the study of ideology, the
intervention of feminism and the emergence of representational theory.
Furthermore as Barbara Klinger (1994) has noted this critical interest in
melodrama (and the techniques deployed in the domestic melodramas
of post-war Hollywood cinema in particular) are epitomised in the interest in the work of Douglas Sirk and more specifically the five key films
Sirk produced whilst working as a director for Universal Studios between
1954 and 1961. The films in question are *Magnificent Obsession* (1954),
All That Heaven Allows (1955), *The Tarnished Angels* (1956), *Written on
the Wind* (1957) and *Imitation of Life* (1961). These five films have become
touchstones for academics concerned with the stylistic characteristics of
melodrama: they have effectively defined what melodrama is understood
to be in Film Studies. As Christine Gledhill observes in her comprehensive
overview of melodrama as an area of academic enquiry, 'through discovery
of Sirk, a genre came into view' (1987: 7); a genre with a particular filmic
style, epitomised in Sirk's films, and Sirk and his films remains firmly positioned at the heart of debate around melodrama in cinema. This means

that an understanding of melodrama as a style necessitates a familiarity with Sirk's filmic techniques. There is, however, a problem here that is sometimes overlooked that needs to be indicated at this early stage. Film Studies academics have tended to imply that the very self-conscious techniques, often regarded as excessive, used by Sirk, are typical of melodramatic style. As Gledhill notes:

> The work of directors, whose exploitation of colour, widescreen, camera movement, had previously been valued for humanist-realist thematics, were now seen as overwrought examples of the bourgeois family melodrama. Stylistic excess had no longer to be defended or justified as the correlative of a coherent vision. It became a positive value, passing from an authorial to a generic trademark and under this rubric the films of Minnelli, Ray, Ophuls, Cukor and Kazan came to stand alongside Sirk to mark the parameters of a new critical field. (ibid.)

However, it is important to remember that although some of the stylistic techniques that Sirk deployed can indeed be seen more widely used in the work of other directors of 1950s Hollywood cinema, Sirk's specific use of these techniques and the intentions that underpinned them are rather specific. Films such as Joshua Logan's *Picnic* (1956) for example have been regarded as revealing conflicts and tensions in 1950s American society though it is also usually acknowledged that the ironic subtext of such films is more inadvertent than intentional. By contrast, Sirk self-consciously, through his own admission, used an elaborate filmic style to undermine the inherent conservatism of the scripts that he was given to work with during his years at Universal. Sirk's intentions therefore were subversive and in many ways his films are atypical of the period rather than the epitome of the Hollywood melodrama. Thomas Schatz, for example, uses the term 'Hollywood Baroque' to describe Sirk's peculiarly elaborate and extravagant style:

> Sirk's interests as a film director, as the premier narrator of female 'weepies' in the 1950s, were based on a style and attitude fundamentally at odds with many, if not most, of the other melodramatists. It certainly takes no more than a few pages of Fanny Hurst's tawdry 1933 bestseller ('Imitation of Life') to realise that in the novel, the narrator actually took the subject matter seriously,

celebrating the American success ethic, romantic love and the nuclear family. Sirk conceived of his subject quite differently than had Hurst – not as a celebration of the American Dream, but as an articulation and ultimately a criticism of it. (1981: 246)

It is perhaps more meaningful to understand Sirk's family melodramas as *emblematic* of both the style and narrative concerns of 1950s Hollywood melodrama. This is not the same as arguing that his films are typical of the period, which is an important point to emphasise. Sirk's films are in many respects atypical but rather become emblematic through a particular use of an ironic *mise-en-scène*, which suggests a critique of bourgeois ideology that reveals wider conflicts and tensions that manifest themselves through the dominant cinema of the period.

Douglas Sirk

Born Dietlef Sierck, Douglas Sirk's early history is widely misrepresented. He was not, as some accounts suggest, Danish and was in fact born in Hamburg.[1] Sierck studied law, philosophy and finally the history of art under the tutelage of the renowned art historian Erwin Panofsky at Hamburg University. Whilst at university he became involved in theatre and in 1922 directed his first play, Bossdorf's *Stationmaster Death*. A left-wing intellectual, well versed in the history of European philosophy and art Sierck was to become a leading figure in progressive German theatre during the coming years. Sierck directed productions by Bertolt Brecht and came under severe criticism by the Nazis in 1933 due to his production of the social critique *The Silver Lake* by Kaiser and Weill. In 1934 he became a director at the German state-run film producers UFA, working alongside a host of directors who would later make careers in Hollywood including Hitchcock, Wilder and Curt Siodmak. During the period between 1934 and 1937 he was to make a succession of films that achieved both popular and critical success that also found favour with the ruling Nazi regime, including *Zu Neuen Ufern* (1937), *Schlussakord* (1936) and his final German film, *La Habanera* (1937). Fleeing Germany at the end of the 1930s, Douglas Sirk, as he was to become known, eventually made his way to Hollywood and worked initially as a director for Columbia from 1942 and from 1946 with Universal.

During a career that lasted over 40 years and includes some 43 films Sirk's output both at UFA and later in Hollywood was to be especially diverse. His first Hollywood production was the war film, *Hitler's Madman* in 1943 and he was to direct several other films within the genre including *Battle Hymn* (1957) and *A Time to Love and a Time to Die* (1958). Sirk also directed thrillers such as *Sleep, My Love* (1948), *Lured* (1947) and *Thunder on the Hill* (1951), the western, *Taza, Son of Cochise* (1954), historical dramas such as *A Scandal in Paris* (1946), *Captain Lightfoot* (1955) and *Sign of the Pagan* (1954) and even comedies and musicals such as *Has Anyone Seen My Gal?* (1952), *Take Me to Town* (1953) and *Meet Me at the Fair* (1953).

What is now regarded as the distinctive Sirkian style was to be fully realised during his years at Universal, working on a succession of projects, characterised, in Paul Willemen and Jon Halliday's words, by 'the grossness and vulgarity of the cliché-ridden plots' (cited in Gledhill 1987: 7). In a series of films that were both huge commercial successes and surreptitious social critiques, Sirk was to bring to bear his experience in avantgarde German theatre, his philosophical interests, concerns as a left-wing intellectual and his aesthetic sensibilities as an art historian.[2]

Through the use of complex and symbolic *mise-en-scène*, irony and pathos and alienation devices borrowed from Brecht, Sirk is now widely regarded as using the conventions of Hollywood cinema to produce critiques of post-war American society.

Sirk and Film Studies

Sirk's critical reception has changed considerably over the years and has resulted in the radical re-evaluation of a relatively obscure contract director, elevating his position to one of the most influential and subversive Hollywood filmmakers of the post-war years. The twists and turns in Sirk's status within the academy are discussed in detail in Barbara Klinger's *Melodrama and Meaning* (1994) and demonstrate very vividly the developments and concerns of Film Studies as an academic discipline during the period of Sirk's 'rediscovery' by the academy. It is inaccurate to suggest that Sirk was completely overlooked prior to his critical re-evaluation by the film theorists of the early 1970s, however. The *Cahiers du cinéma* critics, especially Francois Truffaut, had argued for Sirk's status as an auteur during the late 1950s and several articles during this period point to his singular cinematic style. In 1968 Andrew Sarris identified Sirk as belonging to the second line of auteurs. Though lacking, in Sarris' opinion, a consistently unified stylistic vision, Sirk was nonetheless sufficiently important to be included in his pantheon of Hollywood directors listed in *The American Cinema: Directors and Directions 1922–1968*. A year or so later Jon Halliday tracked down the then retired Sirk and conducted a lengthy interview that was to form the basis of the book *Sirk on Sirk* in 1971. The early, auteurist interest in Sirk had revealed distinctive stylistic techniques in several of his films, duly assisted by his own clear conversancy with film theory and ability to discuss his work in theoretical and reflective terms. Fred Camper's essay 'The Films of Douglas Sirk', published in 1971 in a special edition of *Screen* devoted to Sirk is a good example here. Camper himself notes that, 'no critic has been as perceptive as Sirk himself in articulating some of these themes' (1971: 44). Camper's essay focuses on the aesthetic and narrative patterns in a wide range of films directed by Sirk during his period in Hollywood including *All I Desire, Has Anyone Seen My Gal?* and *A Time to Love and a Time to Die*, as well as the family melodramas *Written on the Wind* and *All That Heaven Allows* that he was to become best known for. However, Klinger notes that as film theory developed during the 1970s and shifted from auteur theory to the study of genre, questions of ideology and representation (and the ideological function of cinema) became ever more important. At this point a sense of a director notable for a diverse range of films diminishes as interest was to be focused on a very specific group of films that Sirk made for Universal, often in collaboration with the producer Ross Hunter in the period between 1954 and 1959. The films in question are primarily domestic family dramas, set in contemporary 1950s America often, though not always, featuring female protagonists.

1950s post-war American society was rather more complicated and contradictory than standard accounts would suggest. Paul Willemen, for example, suggests that Sirk's films reveal a smug and self-satisfied bourgeois worldview which Sirk, the social critic, intends to undermine. In fact, as we noted in chapter one, many films from this period open themselves up to a symptomatic reading and reveal unease and neurosis hidden beneath the surface of respectable society. The end of the Second World War saw a period of rapid economic and industrial development in the US and an increased urban population in the growing suburbs of major cities. The relative independence enjoyed by women in the war years needed to be balanced against the employment needs of men returning home and women were encouraged to return to their more traditional roles as wives and mothers. Women (and teenagers) were consumer groups considered essential to the economic growth of American society during this period and Hollywood cinema tended to reflect this, selling consumerist dreams of luxury and glamour to audiences. This was also a period of political uncertainty with the emergence of the Eastern Bloc and the corresponding American fear of communist totalitarianism. Additionally, the influence of the *Kinsey Report on Human Sexuality* and a growing popular familiarity with Freudianism, resulted in a culture which, paradoxically, celebrated the values of respectable family life and clean living at the same time as a growing awareness of the limitations of these ideals became more accessible to many. The film industry itself was far from immune to the rapid pace of change in post-war America and found itself in the position of competing for audience share with the increasingly popular medium of television. The industries' response to this was firstly to utilise new technological developments such as widescreen and colour more exten- sively as well as exploiting gimmicks such as 3D and secondly to target production at key demographic groupings such as women and teenagers who were identified as key consumers.[3] During the 1950s the production code continued to be enforced even though it was becoming increasingly anachronistic. Paradoxically however, even whilst the code limited what could be depicted or said in a film it also facilitated the emergence of a sophisticated film language that sought, in part at least, to circumvent the restrictions of the code. As Thomas Elsaesser notes,

> the domestic melodrama in colour and widescreen, as it appeared in the 1940s and 1950s is perhaps the most highly elaborated, complex mode of signification that the American cinema has ever produced. (1972: 10)

It is in this context that we should understand the films that are now regarded collectively as family melodramas and in particular the small selection of Douglas Sirk's films that have been singled out for particular critical attention. It was to be this small section of Sirk's directorial career, incorporating no more than five films made towards the end of his career in Hollywood that were to form the basis of his critical reputation both as an auteur and also as the supreme practitioner of the subversive and there- fore progressive Hollywood melodrama.

Magnificent Obsession

Sirk's first melodrama for Universal was to become an unprecedented suc- cess and was to propel Rock Hudson, hitherto a minor movie actor, into Hollywood's A list. Characteristically for Sirk's Hollywood films the story line of *Magnificent Obsession* is extremely implausible and is a remake of John Stahl's 1935 original film of the same name. A reckless playboy, Bob Merrick (Hudson), is the inadvertent cause of a philanthropist Doctor's death. His widow, Helen Phillips (Jane Wyman), is subsequently blinded after a car accident caused by her refusal to accept Bob's apologies. Merrick, racked by guilt, first befriends and then falls in love with the now blinded Helen who is oblivious to his real identity and escorts her around the world in her search for a surgeon who can restore her sight. After a trip to Vienna where she is finally told that her situation is hopeless, Helen disappears without trace. The distraught Bob trains to become a surgeon in an attempt to undo the trail of destruction and unhappiness his reck-lessness has caused. Helen returns to town unexpectedly and Bob realises that he is the only person qualified to perform the pioneering surgery that can save both Helen's life and her sight.

In his interview with Jon Halliday, Sirk was to identify the critical atti-tude that he adopted to the script that would characterise his subversive treatment of the sentimental material he was dealing with:

> You have to do your utmost to hate it – and to love it. My imme-diate reaction to *Magnificent Obsession* was bewilderment and discouragement. But still I was attracted by something irrational in it. Something mad, in a way – well obsessed, because this is a damned crazy story if ever there was one. (1997: 109)

All That Heaven Allows

Originally conceived in some haste to capitalise on the huge commercial success of *Magnificent Obsession*, the film reunites Rock Hudson and Jane Wyman. *All That Heaven Allows* is widely considered to be the film in which Sirk is first able to fully realise the potential for social critique afforded by what some critics have seen as the banal scripts offered to him by Universal. The claim that Sirk deploys Brechtian techniques in his main-stream Hollywood output is also frequently evidenced by reference to this film. The film was an immense inspiration to the German filmmaker Rainer Werner Fassbinder who used it as the basis for his own *Fear Eats the Soul* (1973). *All That Heaven Allows* is the story of a wealthy suburban widow Cary Scott (Wyman) who develops a relationship with her gardener, a work-ing class, and younger, freethinking non-conformist, Ron Kirby, played by Rock Hudson. The relationship between the two becomes the focus of local gossip amongst Cary's small-minded neighbours. It is, however, Cary's two

FIGURE 4 Mitch and Marylee in *Written on the Wind*

grown-up children who most object to her plans for marriage and they present their mother with an ultimatum: either she gives up her younger lover or lose her children. The anguished Cary chooses respectability rather than love and gives up Ron. The futility of this act of self sacrifice is revealed when her children announce that they are both leaving home anyway and that Cary will need to sell the family home and be left alone. A freak accident (Ron falling from a snowy cliff and becoming gravely ill) reunites the couple and Cary realising the error of her ways, is left nursing the incapacitated Ron back to health.

Written on the Wind

In Sirk's words: 'It was a piece of social criticism, of the rich and the spoiled and of the American family' (1997: 130). *Written on the Wind*, an expose into the corrupting influences of wealth and privilege, was to form the blueprint for subsequent family melodramas such as Mark Robson's *Peyton Place* (1957) as well as a generation of prime-time television soap operas such as *Dallas*, *Dynasty*, *The Colbys* and *Falcon Crest*. Told in flashback, the film recounts the events that result in the tragic death of Kyle Hadley (Robert Stack), alcoholic and impotent heir to the Hadley oil empire. The story concerns the friendship between the wealthy Kyle and his lifelong friend Mitch Wayne (Rock Hudson), who form a love triangle with Kyle's new bride, Lucy (Lauren Bacall). An added complication to this already inflammatory constellation of characters is introduced by Kyle's sister, Marylee (Dorothy Malone). Marylee is in love with Mitch, though these sentiments are unrequited, and substitutes her feelings for Mitch through illicit encounters with local men. Whilst Kyle is impotent and drowns his frustrations in drink, Marylee is presented as a nymphomaniac who brings her family's name into disrepute. She is ultimately the inadvertent cause of her father's demise, who literally dies with shame as a result of her actions. When Kyle discovers that his wife is pregnant, he presumes that Mitch is the father and in a drunken rage shoots himself. Marylee vindictively accuses Mitch of murdering her brother and the true sequence of events are not revealed until a dramatic court scene. The film has a peculiarly ambiguous ending with Lucy and Mitch driving away from the Hadley mansion and Marylee, stripped of her sexual independence, dressed in a conservative suit, caressing an unmistakeably phallic model of an oil pump, beneath a portrait of her dead father. As Sirk notes,

> The end of *Written on the Wind* is highly significant as far as this is concerned: Malone has lost everything. I have put up a sign there indicating this – Malone, alone, sitting there, hugging that goddamned oil well, having nothing. The oil well which is, I think, a rather frightening symbol of American society. (1997: 133)

The Tarnished Angels
The least typical of Sirk's films during this period, *The Tarnished Angels* reunites the love triangle of *Written on the Wind*, Rock Hudson, Dorothy Malone and Robert Stack in an adaptation of William Faulkner's novel *Pylon*. Filmed in black and white rather than the luxurious, widescreen Technicolor of Sirk's other Universal melodramas, the film is set in depression-era America where a celebrated fighter pilot Roger Schumann has been reduced to performing as a daredevil pilot to make ends meet and support himself and his wife Laverne (Malone). Hudson plays a reporter, Burke Devlin who becomes fascinated by the lives of the couple and increasingly romantically interested in Laverne. The film very vividly illustrates Sirk's interest in failure as a narrative theme, especially in the characterisation of the doomed fighter pilot Schumann who crashes his plane towards the end of the film. In Sirk's observation, Schumann is 'seeking his identity, a man standing on very uncertain ground. The ground doesn't give him any

security, he is reaching for a certainty in the air – a crazy idea, and a grand one, I think' (1997: 137). The difference in inflection in Sirk's own view of the source material for *The Tarnished Angels* (he describes it as 'grand') is interesting here and is an issue that we will return to later. The film however is perhaps best known as Barbara Klinger notes for a scene where 'Laverne parachutes from a plane as her dress blows up and conveniently reveals her lower torso for an extended period of time' (1993: 151).

Imitation of Life

Sirk's final film for Universal (and his last film in Hollywood) is also perhaps his most bitter, pessimistic and overt comment on American society and values. Once again the film is a remake of an earlier film by John Stahl.[4] The film concerns itself with the tribulations of two single mothers – one white, Lora Meredith (Lana Turner), and one black, Annie Johnson (Juanita Moore), and their two daughters Susie and Sarah Jane (played by Sandra Dee and Susan Kohner respectively). Lora is a struggling actress and Annie becomes her maid and constant companion. The story charts the rags to riches rise of Lora's character along with the development of the daughters of the two women. Whilst Lora's daughter, Susie, has a life representing many young girls' dreams, Annie's daughter, Sarah Jane, is deeply troubled and refuses to accept her subordinate status as both poor and black. Sarah Jane becomes increasingly rebellious and tries to 'pass for white'. When this strategy is no longer feasible she rejects her mother and the security of Lora's luxurious home and becomes a showgirl in a nightclub. Her mother Annie quickly falls gravely ill and decides that she must find Sarah Jane in order to reconcile their differences. Finding Sarah Jane dancing in a nightclub, Annie pleads with her daughter in perhaps the most affecting and genuinely moving moment in any of Sirk's films. Sarah Jane, however, refuses to accept her mother's pleas and Annie returns home and dies. This sets the scene for one of the most memorable and best-known sequences in any of Sirk's films: Annie's funeral. A lavishly mounted and extraordinarily extravagant affair, attended by a guest list of extras including famed Hollywood producers, agents, actors and directors, the funeral is centred on a performance by the renowned gospel singer Mahalia Jackson. The scene suggests that it is only in death that Annie can achieve the level of status and recognition that Lora Meredith, her white mistress, has enjoyed in life. The film ends with Sarah Jane's appearance at the funeral, literally throwing herself on her dead mother's coffin. Sirk observed that the character of Sarah Jane was his specific interest in the film:

The only interesting thing is the Negro angle: the Negro girl trying to escape her condition, sacrificing to her status in society her bonds of friendship, family, etc., and rather trying to vanish into the imitation world of vaudeville. The imitation of life is not the real life. Lana Turner's life is a very cheap imitation. The girl (Susan Kohner) is choosing the imitation of life instead of being a Negro. The picture is a piece of social criticism – of both black and white. You can't escape what you are. (1997: 148)

The progressive Sirk

During the 1970s Sirk's status and significance was to be substantially elevated. No longer regarded as merely a skilled manipulator of the poetic or stylistic potential of cinematic aesthetics, increasingly he was to be identified as a director who deployed cinematic *mise-en-scène* in a strategic fashion to subvert the apparent meanings of a film and to critique bourgeois ideology. During the early to mid-1970s a surprising reversal seems to take place in the ways in which Sirk's films are understood. Working within the constraints of what were seen as the deeply reactionary narrative and generic conventions of the woman's film and the 'weepie', Sirk is now regarded as a progressive auteur using the conservative form of the romance to his own subversive ends.

The critical re-evaluation of Sirk's films, which commenced in the late 1960s, was to continue throughout the early years of the 1970s. As already observed in chapter one, Elsaesser had established the terms of reference for the discussion of melodrama in the Hollywood cinema in the 1950s in generic and stylistic terms, and his position was to be adopted by a succession of critics during the early 1970s, most notably, Fred Camper, Laura Mulvey and Paul Willemen. Willemen in particular is especially significant as he was to identify some of the key features of Sirk's filmic style that were to become central to the academic account of his significance. Equally importantly Willemen, like many of his contemporaries, was interested in the techniques of Bertolt Brecht and argued that there were clear parallels in the filmic strategies that Sirk deployed in this respect.

Brecht was perhaps the most important German dramatist of the twentieth century and his ideas have become central to our understanding of what experimental theatre is. As a politically motivated dramatist, Brecht rejected the dominant mode of realism in contemporary theatre.

He believed that theatre had the potential to deal with the major themes of human existence and should be concerned with enlightening an audience and motivating political change; for Brecht drama should be didactic.[5] The dramatic strategy adopted to realise this goal was the deployment of what we now call alienation or distanciation, Brecht himself described it as the 'alienation effect' or 'A effect'.

Seeing the realism of late nineteenth- and early twentieth-century theatre as intrinsically bourgeois, he proposed a new 'realistic' form of theatre that would enlighten audiences to the reality of the conditions of their existence and therefore motivate political and social change. Brecht was to become a figure of renewed interest for critics in the early 1970s because of these techniques and his stylistic challenge to dominant ideology; he indicates the direction that a progressive drama would take and for scholars searching for the 'progressive text' therefore Brechtian techniques provide evidence of progressive status.

Sirk's background in theatre played a part in the identification of Brechtian techniques in his films. He had directed Brecht's *Threepenny Opera* in Berlin in 1929, for example, and it was assumed therefore that he was not just familiar but also sympathetic to the concerns of Brecht's drama. In 1971 Willemen's essay 'Distanciation and Douglas Sirk' positions Sirk as emerging from and belonging to the European artistic avant-garde. He sees Sirk as producing cinema that questions the illusion of reality that characterises the filmic strategies of the Classical Hollywood cinema. Willemen identifies Sirk's aesthetic style as being especially significant and suggests that it is inspired by artistic movements, most notably German expressionism and symbolism, though he is careful to qualify this claim:

> for Sirk, such prescriptions represent a source of inspiration and become no more than echoes, detectable in his magnification of emotionality, his use of pathos, choreography and music, reverberating within the mirror-ridden walls of a Sirkian décor. (1971: 64)

Later in the essay Willemen identifies some of the techniques and devices deployed by Sirk that for subsequent critics were to become characteristic of his filmic style. He notes Sirk's deliberate use of visual symbols as representatives of characters, the use of long shots, giving the sets a stage-like impression, the use of extravagant colour schemes and choreography as 'a direct expression of character' (1971: 65). He also notes the self-conscious use of cliché in Sirk's films, suggesting that the stylisation of Sirk's extravagant *mise-en-scène* and his manipulation of the conventions of exaggerated emotion and sentiment so evident in the Universal melodramas, reaches the point of parody: 'a deer and a Christmas tree are symbols for nature; a mink coat stands for success; a red-lit cabaret stand for depravity; a red dress and fast cars stand for loose living and irresponsibility' (1971: 66). Willemen notes that this parodic style should not be regarded as comedic but rather as a device that is designed to create a distance between the text and the critical audience for Sirk's films. Importantly here Willemen also notes that these self-conscious techniques were not necessarily evident to the audience for which these films were intended.

> On the contrary, he mercilessly implicates the audience in the action. (Ample proof of this can be found in the audience's near hysterical reactions to his films involving abundant tears and/or self-protective laughter.) Such reactions seem to indicate that the distance Sirk is referring to is not necessarily perceived by the audience. (1971: 64)

In the essay 'Towards and Analysis of the Sirkian System', Willemen identifies more specifically the similarities between the techniques used by Brecht in the theatre and those used by Sirk in his Universal pictures. In particular he discusses Brecht's early technique known as the *boomerang effect*:

> Brecht presented the theatre public with the image of life that it wanted to see on the stage, but in order to denounce the unreality of such an image, to denounce its ideological character. (1972: 128)

Willemen argues that a similar effect is achieved in Sirk's 1950s melodramas in which 'he depicted a society which appeared to be strong and healthy, but which in fact was exhausted and torn apart by collective neuroses' (1972: 133). In Halliday's interview Sirk was to note that he self-consciously used Brechtian techniques in his choice of film titles:

> Take *All That Heaven Allows*: I just put this title there like a cup of tea, following Brecht's recipe. The studio loved this title, they thought it meant that you could have everything you wanted. I meant it exactly the other way round. As far as I'm concerned, heaven is stingy. (1997: 140)

The idea that Sirk's films reveal hidden societal tensions was to become central to critical appraisal of his oeuvre and wider discussion of the cinema of 1950s Hollywood more generally which has subsequently been regarded as revealing the symptoms of an underlying crisis in postwar American society.

Willemen notes in his essay that Sirk's films were widely misunderstood when they were first released and points to Sirk's own commentary on the matter in which he suggests that the ironic nature of his many of his films was frequently lost on industry professionals and audiences alike. Certainly contemporary film reviews were almost uniformly critical. Reviewers tended to regard Sirk's films as either stark examples of failed naturalism due to their lavish sets, artificial lighting and garish colours or as indicators of Hollywood's inability to deal with complex issues with sensitivity, preferring instead to simplify and sentimentalise. As Barbara Klinger notes, the extravagant *mise-en-scène* and stylisation of Sirk's melodramas were singled out for particular criticism:

> *Written of the Wind*'s décor was 'luxurious and the colour is conspicuously strong, even though it gets no closer to Texas – either geographically or in spirit – than a few locations near Hollywood'. (1994: 78)

Similarly *Imitation of Life* was condemned for 'its lavish colour production, its tear-jerking qualities, and the irresistible circumstance that Lana Turner wears more than one million dollars worth of jewellery and a wardrobe of equal opulence and bad taste' (1994: 79). Such contemporary reviews are far removed from the positions adopted by intellectuals like Willemen during the early 1970s for whom Sirk's films become exemplars of modernist anti-naturalism, full of examples of Brechtian-inspired distanciation techniques; films that, it was argued, are in fact rich with ironic subtexts and subversive critiques of bourgeois ideology.

In his essay Willemen moves on to identify five key aspects that epitomise Sirk's filmic style drawing on a wider number of films than those that would later be generally regarded as the canonical texts. Firstly, Willemen points out that what he describes as 'displacements and discontinuities in plot construction' (1972: 131) recur in Sirk's films. He refers here to Sirk's strategy of creating supporting characters in films that have a greater narrative significance than the lead protagonists. Kyle and Marylee Hadley in *Written on the Wind*, for example, are revealed as the 'hidden' leads of the film and likewise Sarah Jane in *Imitation of Life*. Secondly, he notes 'contradictions in characterisation' (ibid.) illustrated by Kyle Hadley in *Written on the Wind* and by Taza in *Taza, Son of Cochise*. A clearer example is provided by Sarah Jane in *Imitation of Life*, a split character in the classic Sirkian sense; neither entirely black nor white, she struggles to resist pressures to conform to society's expectations of her within the film, ultimately by rejecting her mother and the security of her home. Thirdly, Willemen identifies Sirk's use of ironic framing and camera positioning. Using examples from *All That Heaven Allows*, he notes that shot constructions make explicit the rift between Cary Scott and her two children. As we will observe later in this chapter, there are abundant examples of this technique in Sirk's films. Fourthly, he notes 'formal negations of ideological notions inherent in the script' (ibid.). This rather confusing expression refers to Sirk's use of cliché and parody, devices that undermine the apparently reactionary storylines that Sirk consistently subverted in his melodramas in order to distance audiences from the ideologies embedded in the narratives. Willemen illustrates this by using the example of the banal metaphorical comparison of spirituality to a domestic electricity supply used in *Magnificent Obsession*. Finally, he notes the ironic use of camera movement arguing that long and mid-shots are frequently used in Sirk's films to create a sense of distance, giving the action, as he had noted previously, a theatrical quality. He notes, however, that the camera is also constantly mobile and that this simultaneously emotionally engages the audience.

Sirkian style

Drawing together the stylistic features of Sirk's melodramas identified by a wide range of theorists from Sirk himself to Elsaesser, Willemen, Mulvey, Camper, Truffaut and Schatz it is possible to identify a range of thematic and narrative patterns that collectively become emblematic of the Sirkian style. Similar techniques can be seen employed by several of Sirk's contemporaries such as Nicholas Ray, Billy Wilder and Vincente Minnelli though these patterns are most apparent in Sirk's films. We shall consider briefly these here.

In much of Sirk's cinema long- and mid-shots are far more regularly used than close-ups. This is especially apparent in both *Written on the Wind* and *Imitation of Life*. The use of long-shots creates a very visible distance between the audience and the action on the screen giving the films a very theatrical quality. Long-shots additionally enable the possibility of

FIGURE 5 Emotional distance represented visually in *Written on the Wind*

elaborately structured visual compositions within the frame giving the audience the opportunity to see several characters at the same time.

Widescreen, deep-focus photography of the kind used by Sirk in almost all of his most celebrated melodramas makes it possible to illustrate the emotional distance between characters in physical terms and this is a technique that he was to take full advantage of. In *Written on the Wind* for example, Marylee professes her unrequited love for Mitch whilst driving a flashy red sports car. The emotional rift between the two characters and Mitch's lack of sexual interest in Marylee who he claims to love 'like a brother' is illustrated by a mid-shot of the couple through the windscreen of the car in which both characters seem to be pushed to either edge of the frame.

The setting for Sirk's melodramas is usually the affluent middle-class American home, a setting in which décor plays a part as important as the characters in carrying meaning. In Elsaesser's words, 'the setting of the family melodrama almost by definition is the middle-class home, filled with objects ... that becomes increasingly suffocating' (1987: 61). In Sirk's films the décor and objects that surround characters seem overburdened with meaning and significance, everything in the frame means something giving the images that Sirk constructs at points a rather stifling impression. In *All That Heaven Allows*, discussed in greater detail in his essay, Cary is frequently depicted surrounded by meaning-laden objects in her luxurious domestic environment.

A further common feature are mirrors, used as a significant feature of the *mise-en-scène* in Sirk's films with some degree of regularity. Sirk suggested that mirrors were of interest because they produce an image that seems to represent the person looking into the mirror when in fact what they see is their exact opposite. In Sirk's films we see characters looking in mirrors when they are conforming to society's rules, when they are playing a role, when they are deluding themselves. Mirrors, then, represent both illusion and delusion in his films, and were to become such an emblematic device in Sirk's melodramas that examples are almost too numerous to mention. One of the most vivid cases, however, occurs towards the end of *Imitation of Life* when the black housekeeper, Annie, realising that her death is imminent, tries to forge a final reconciliation with her wayward daughter Sarah Jane who tries to 'pass for white' as a showgirl. Annie pleads with her furious daughter in the dressing room of a nightclub trying to encourage her to accept her identity as black and her mother's love. Sarah Jane is completely unaware of Annie's illness and the cruelty of her rejection of her mother gives the scene an extraordinary emotional power. The emotional crescendo of the scene has Sarah Jane screaming, 'I'm white, I'm white' whilst her distraught face, and that of her mother's, is caught in the reflection of the dressing room mirror.

Another visual device used by Sirk has become known as 'frames within frames'. Characters are often seen contained within mirror frames, doorways, windows, pictures frames and decorative screens. These devices once again suggest that characters are isolated or confined in their lonely worlds, or oppressed by their environments. Elsaesser illustrates this point with an example from *Written on the Wind*:

> Robert Stack in *Written on the Wind*, standing by the window he has just opened to get some fresh air into an extremely heavy family atmosphere, hears of Lauren Bacall expecting a baby. His misery becomes eloquent by the way he squeezes himself into the frame of the half-open window, every word his wife says to him bringing torment to his lacerated soul and racked body. (1987: 59)

Colour is used both symbolically and expressively in Sirk's films. The relatively new technology of the Technicolor process enabled filmmakers to fully realise the expressive potential of colour in film in the 1950s. The

FIGURE 6 Cary, confined by convention and the window frame in *All That Heaven Allows*

harsh, garish colours of *Written on the Wind* for example were consciously chosen to emphasise the surface of objects and the centrality of materialism to the film. Marylee's red sports car, the red telephone and vivid red lilies in her bedroom all symbolise her sexual aggression. Similarly in *Interlude* one of Sirk's less well-known melodramas in which June Alyson plays Helen Banning, a young American secretary who falls in love with a charismatic and married orchestral conductor, Antonio Fischer (played by Rossano Brazzi), the psychological illness of Brazzi's wife, Reni Fischer, is made explicit by the oppressively decadent colour schemes of the music room in which she is first seen in the shadowy reflection created by the polished surface of a grand piano.

Like colour, lighting is used expressively in Sirk's films. Through the use of shadows and coloured filters, extremely artificial lighting effects are achieved that represent the mood of a scene or a character rather than aiming for more naturalistic lighting. Marylee's nighttime rendezvous with Mitch in *Written on the Wind* is set against a vivid cobalt blue backlight that symbolises the cold reception that she is receiving and also the artifice of her attempts at seduction. In *Magnificent Obsession* the scenes set in Austria, during which Helen seeks medical help to restore her sight, are shot almost entirely as nighttime, both expressing the character's increasing despair and symbolising her loss of sight. In a scene from *All That Heaven Allows*, Cary has a tearful conversation with her daughter Kay who has been the subject of ridicule as a result of her mother's relationship with the gardener Ron Kirby. The scene takes place in Kay's bedroom which is dominated by a circular oriel window through which an extremely unnaturalistic, rainbow light shines on the couple. This lighting effect is reminiscent of the effect of a stained-glass window and creates an expressionistic metaphor for the conversation and its implications. As Cary listens to her tearful daughter she realises that she must end her relationship with Ron. The lighting effect here symbolises Cary's 'revelation' that her love for Ron is doomed.

Central to Sirk's aesthetic vision, however, is irony and he is most consistently recognised for his use of an ironic *mise-en-scène*. The settings, décor, lighting, music and camera framing of Sirk's films often seem to contradict or place an alternative emphasis on what is taking place within the narrative. In simple terms, the story or the characters seem to be saying one thing and the *mise-en-scène* seems to be saying something else and drawing our attention to the irony of the character's delusions. Irony, then, becomes a central component of Sirk's status as a progressive or subversive auteur; he appropriates the conventions of the Hollywood romance and through the deployment of an ironic *mise-en-scène* uses a popular form of cinema as a tool for social critique.

Sirk's ironic *mise-en-scène* is perhaps best illustrated through his self-conscious use of cliché. Sirk frequently deploys clichéd imagery and scenarios to seemingly draw attention to their very artificiality. For Sirk, this is yet another Brechtian device, reminding an audience, sensitive to such ironising techniques, that they were witnessing a fiction. In *All That Heaven Allows* for example, Sirk uses clichéd symbols of nature to the point that they approach parody. Ron Kirby is seen feeding a tamed deer, which also appears in the miraculously artificial panorama revealed when the nurse pulls back the shutters at the Old Mill at the end of the film. The very artifice of this final fantasy of nature calls into question the happy resolution that the narrative of the film seems to suggest.

Narrative themes

It has often been said that Sirk, as a contract director, was often given clichéd and derivative material to work with that he had no control over. Thomas Schatz, for example, characterizes Sirk's Hollywood career:

> Sirk's films were assigned to him by studio bosses and he retired just at the point when he might have taken charge. Conceivably, though, personal control over his projects might well have undermined Sirk's particular talents. He was one of those rare directors who thrived on adversity, whose best work was done with outrageous scripts and dehumanising working conditions. (1981: 246–7)

It is notable that the films aimed at a primarily female audience (*All That Heaven Allows, Imitation of Life* and *Magnificent Obsession*) or those based on popular women's fiction (the work of Fanny Hurst for example) are singled out for particular criticism. Sirk himself demonstrates distaste for this kind of source material verging on contempt for both the scripts and the audiences for such films, describing them as 'trash' and 'crazy'. Likewise, critics like Willemen, Halliday and Schatz also decry the supposedly 'banal' or 'sentimental' nature of material aimed at women, priviledging a critical reading position afforded by familiarity with the supposedly subversive intentions of Sirk whilst regarding an uncritical, empathetic, response to these films as inferior. By contrast, Sirk speaks of the 'grand' themes of failure in films such as *The Tarnished Angels* and *Written on the Wind* both of which feature male protagonists. In both the critical accounts and first hand testimony of Sirk there is a very apparent failure to either acknowledge or engage seriously with the pleasures or political significances of the emotional responses that Sirk's most popular films so clearly provoke in audiences. This is a problem surrounding the discussion of melodrama that Linda Williams was to later acknowledge and is a subject that we will return to in chapter three.

In actual fact as Universal's 'star' director, Sirk was often able to rework scripts, in his own words 'bending' the narrative to incorporate his own specific interests:

I became a kind of house director of Universal. Conditions were not perfect, but when I complained about a story, they would say to me, 'If you can get a star, great; you can have more money and pick a better story.' But at least I was allowed to work on the material – so that I restructured, to some extent, some of the rather impossible scripts of the films I had to direct. (1997: 97)

Through his revisions and rewrites of scripts a succession of distinctive themes start to emerge in the Universal melodramas, and we shall consider some of these here.

One consistent thread is blindness. As Sirk notes:

I have always been intrigued by the problems of blindness ... What I think would be extremely interesting here would be to try and confront problems of this kind via a medium – the cinema – which itself is only concerned with things seen. It is this contrast between a world where words have only a limited importance and another world where they are nearly everything that inspires my passionate interest. (1997: 111)

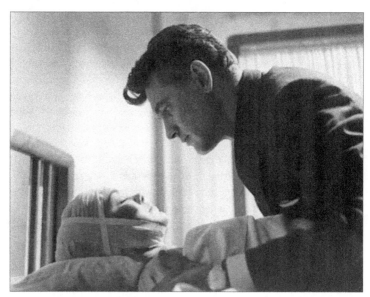

FIGURE 7 Reformed playboy Bob Merrick's bedside vigil in *Magnificent Obsession*

Blindness has been identified by both Jon Halliday and Fred Camper as a recurrent theme in Sirk's films. It is used, either literally, as in *Magnificent Obsession* where Helen is accidentally blinded or, more often, in a metaphorical sense. Frequently Sirk's films deal with characters who seem oblivious to their isolated or helpless conditions and cannot see the possibility of change. In *All That Heaven Allows* for example, Cary gives up Ron in ignorance of the fact that her children no longer need her and that her act of motherly self-sacrifice will inevitably result in her own isolation.

Circularity and hopelessness are also common narrative motifs in Sirk's melodramas; characters seem to repeat the same mistakes, not only oblivious to these patterns, but also seemingly unable to escape their conditions. Sirk noted an interest in failure and hopelessness that inspired the production of both *Written on the Wind* and *The Tarnished Angels*: 'Failure and being blocked is indeed one of the few themes which interests me passionately. Success is not interesting to me' (1997: 133). The implicit suggestion in a film such as *Imitation of Life*, for example, being that there is no escape from prejudice and social control. Annie the black housekeeper dies without any reconciliation with her daughter. This sense of fatalistic circularity demonstrated in the narrative means that Sirk's films are often – ironically, given their superficially 'happy' endings – very pessimistic in their outlook.

An important element of Sirk's narrative thematics is the so-called *deus ex machina*, a term he uses in his interview with Jon Halliday. The term often has derogatory connotations akin to those associated with 'divine intervention' and originates in the Classical Greek theatre referring to the practice where actors playing gods would be attached to a winch-like machine and suspended over the action towards the end of a play. In these circumstances the gods would appear to intervene to resolve difficult situations and bring the play to a satisfactory conclusion. In modern usage the term refers to the use of contrived coincidences and circumstances that occur to resolve a narrative. In Sirk's melodramas there are many such instances. *Magnificent Obsession*, for example, has a narrative that is based around a sequence of improbable events; Bob Merrick inadvertently is the cause of the death of Helen's fiancée, then is the cause of her blindness, and finally, through training to become a pioneering surgeon, saves both her sight and her life. Similarly in *All That Heaven Allows* Ron's accident, caused in part due to Cary's sudden arrival at the Old Mill, is also the catalyst for their reunion. The endings of Sirk's melodramas, due in part to the contrivances of the *deus ex machina* resolutions, often feel rather artificial, and a recurring feature in the films is the 'false happy ending'. In some cases, as in *All That Heaven Allows* and *Written on the Wind*, the seemingly happy endings feel rather unsatisfactory and give the impression that they have been tacked on through necessity rather than design. Sirk acknowledged the nature of these, so-called, happy endings: 'you've got to have a happy end even in the most goddam awful situations' (1997: 152) and argued that they were there in part at least due to the requirements of the studio and the restrictions imposed as a result of the production code: 'Of course, I had to go by the rules, avoid experiments, stick to family fare, have "happy endings" and so on' (1997: 97). However, given these restrictions Sirk still suggested that the happy endings of his melodramas were self-consciously artificial, that he was in fact deliberately creating false happy endings that draw ironic attention to the tensions and inconsistencies within the conventionalised storylines of his films: 'you don't believe the happy ending and you're not really supposed to' (1997: 151).

Case study: All That Heaven Allows

As already noted, *All That Heaven Allows* was produced, primarily, to capitalise on the phenomenal success of *Magnificent Obsession*, featuring the earlier film's two leads, the established star Jane Wyman and the emerging star Rock Hudson. Given the conditions of its production and also the fact that Sirk himself, when interviewed by Jon Halliday, could scarcely remember the film at all, it is rather ironic that *All That Heaven Allows* has become something of a touchstone not just for academics concerned with Sirk's style but also for subsequent filmmakers inspired by Sirk's techniques. The narrative of the film is deceptively simple, whilst at an aesthetic level it is complexly structured and elaborately stylised. Sirk, commenting on the film during a BBC interview in 1979, described it as containing a lot of his 'handwriting',[6] notably the elaborate use of mirrors and other visual symbols, as well as his use of literary references in narratives. The film is significant because it elegantly encapsulates many of Sirk's key stylistic techniques and narrative preoccupations and is therefore well suited to a case study for analysis of the Sirkian style and over time has become peculiarly susceptible to a multitude of readings. For our purposes, *All That Heaven Allows* illustrates four key stylistic and narrative issues; subversive social critique, Cary's oppression, the alternative offered by Ron Kirby and the problematic 'happy ending', each of which will be considered in turn.

The film can firstly be regarded as a subversive social critique of suburban American attitudes and prejudices. The opening title sequence locates the film very clearly in affluent, smalltown America with a craning, panoramic, aerial shot of the fictional town of Stoningham, radiating from the steeple of the local church. This opening image is accompanied by Frank Skinner's musical score, which takes the poignant melody of Franz Liszt's piano piece, *Consolation No.3* and reworks it as the basis of a lush symphonic score with the sweeping romantic proportions of Rachmaninov. The musical accompaniment makes the romantic content of the film immediately apparent and it is this musical theme that will be returned to over and over again throughout the film at moments of dramatic significance. Whilst the opening sequence offers the audience an idyllic image of suburban America it is not long before the rather less attractive sides of smalltown life are revealed. From the outset we understand that Cary Scott is recently widowed and has two grown up children at college. Left alone in her large home she is becoming lonely and is invited by her friend Sarah for drinks at the Stoningham Country Club. Although reticent, Cary agrees. The notion of the country club, clichéd shorthand for elitism and privilege, is presented as the social focus of the small community and we quickly realise that it is also a locus of gossip and snobbery epitomised in the character of Mona Plash. The country club is also the location for two dramatic sequences that illustrate the community's attitude towards Cary as a widow, and later, to Cary and Ron as a couple. In the first scene set in the country club, Cary arrives with her escort, the elderly hypochondriac, Harvey (Conrad Nagel). Harvey is single and therefore regarded as a suitable partner for the widowed Cary by both her children and the wider community. Cary's daughter Kay, for example, identifies through reference to Freud that Harvey is an appropriate consort primarily because he offers no sexual threat. At the club, however, Cary's status is questioned by the community, symbolised by Mona. Cary chooses to wear a red evening gown, illustrating her new status as a single and available woman, a choice that has already been commented upon by Ned her son. At the club Mona echoes Ned's unease with the remark 'There's nothing like red for attracting attention.' After this exchange Cary is asked to dance by Howard Hoffer, a married lothario who makes a clumsy and rejected attempt to seduce her. Cary returns home, disillusioned by her unsatisfactory evening only to receive an equally unwelcome doorstep marriage proposal from Harvey, which she also declines. Harvey suggests that companionship is all that Cary and he could possibly want at their time of life. These scenes illustrate Cary's predicament as a middle-aged widow in her community; either the lecherous and adulterous attentions of a married man or sterile companionship from an elderly single man seem to be the only options available to her.

Rather than choosing between Harvey and Howard, Cary falls in love with her gardener Ron Kirby, a younger man and, equally importantly, a tradesman and therefore her social inferior. This choice, and its consequences, brings the prejudice of both Cary's community and family into stark relief. The second scene at the country club illustrates this vividly. After Cary and Ron have received a frosty reception from Cary's children they visit the club on Sarah's suggestion. As Cary leaves her home with Ron she notices his car (a tradesman's van) and, in a vain hope of preserving some vestige of her respectability, suggests that they arrive in her, rather more suitable, family car. Cary's face, shot in close-up, demonstrates her concern. Ron, seemingly oblivious to her concerns, refuses her request. The scene at the club opens with the members peering through net curtains, excitedly awaiting the arrival of the couple. Long shots are used at this point to distance the audience from the characters. There are no point of view shots at this stage so that the audience is not privileged to the crowd's view through the window which makes their gossip and evident excitement appear simultaneously threatening and ludicrous. Once Cary and Ron arrive at the club they become the focus of the group's voyeuristic attentions. Mona, dressed in emerald green satin, symbolising her jealous character, is once again positioned at the centre of the community's scandalised responses, evidently taking pleasure in Cary's discomfort with cutting remarks drawing attention to Ron's subordinate social status, such as 'Oh my dear he's fascinating. And that tan! I suppose from working outdoors. Though I'm sure he's handy indoors too.' The scene culminates with an aggressive physical encounter between Ron and the drunken Howard who confronts Cary about her previous rejection of him claiming that Cary had put on 'The perfect lady act. Making me apologize. If I'd have known then what I know now the story would have had a different ending.' The aggressive encounter between Ron and Howard only provides more fuel for Mona's gossip: 'Cary and Howard, I'd never have thought it ... Howard as the earthy type, but you seem to attract that don't you, Cary?'

Returning from the ugly scene that confirms Stoningham's prejudice, Cary is finally, and brutally, confronted with the spectre of snobbery in her own home in a scene with her son Ned. Ned accuses his mother of being distracted by 'a handsome set of muscles' and says that she must choose between Ron and her family. The stylistic elements of the scene illustrate the forces conspiring against Ron and Cary's happiness. The scene takes place in Cary's lounge, which is backlit with a highly artificial blue light. Cary is shot, seemingly trapped, against a decorative screen, cast in shadow, with only her face illuminated by high-key lighting. Ned, shot from behind in shadow, looms threateningly over his mother as he presents his ultimatum.

The first part of the film presents Cary as a victim; oppressed by the rigid codes of her society, by her gender position as widow, wife and mother, by the restrictions placed on her by her family and by her own attitudes. This sense of Cary's oppression is vividly expressed through *mise-en-scène* and especially the domestic environment in which she is most consistently placed. The Scott's home is presented as a luxurious mausoleum for Cary's dead husband. The lounge, for example, is dominated by a huge fireplace, adorned with the deceased Mr Scott's sporting trophies and a similarly vast, marbled mirror covering the whole wall. This sense that Cary's home is a tomb is made explicit in an early conversation between Kay and Cary. Kay tells her mother that she should re-enter the social world and perhaps find a suitable partner. Kay tells her mother, 'I don't subscribe to the old Egyptian custom of walling the wife up along with the rest of the dead husband's possessions … of course that doesn't happen anymore.' Cary's response to this remark is telling; 'Doesn't it? Well perhaps not in Egypt.'

Cary's oppressed and isolated state is also expressed visually through the repeated use of mirrors and reflections. After her first encounter with Ron, Cary is seen at her dressing table gazing at her own reflection. At this point her children arrive home and are introduced, visually, caught in the mirror's reflection with their mother, emphasising the oppressive nature of their relationship. Later Cary is seen playing the piano in her lounge, the music stand of the piano is replaced by a mirror, reflecting Cary's image back at herself, as she sits in splendid isolation. The Scott residence seems through these aspects of the *mise-en-scène* to be full of cold reflective surfaces that painfully illustrate Cary's isolation and alienation from her environment. The key narrative motif of the television salesman is also introduced to both demonstrate the shallow substitutes for love offered to Cary and to illustrate the trajectory of her relationship with Ron. Embedded in the motif of the television is another ironic and sly subtext; at a historical point at which television was challenging the dominance of cinema, a critique of television – as a substitute for companionship – is introduced.

FIGURE 8 Cary trapped in her 'Egyptian Tomb' in *All That Heaven Allows*

Sara advises Cary to buy a television, a suggestion that she resolutely refuses. Sara's response questions Cary's thinking: 'Why? Because it's supposed to be the last refuge of the lonely woman?' In the same scene Ron, Cary's true alternative to loneliness, arrives unexpectedly to whisk her away to dinner. Later on, in the midst of Ron and Cary's romance, the television salesman arrives, once more, at Cary's door. She turns him away telling him that she is too busy to watch television. The bitter irony of this scene only becomes apparent later, in perhaps the most discussed sequence in the whole film which most fully encapsulates Cary's oppression through the full range of Sirkian filmic devices.

Cary, finally realising her impossible situation, splits up with Ron and returns to her old life as a lonely widow. The sequence opens with a short scene of clichéd Christmas-card sentimentality that illustrates Cary's isolation. Outside snow is falling and children are seen singing carols on a sleigh. These idealised images of Christmas are inter-cut with a mid-shot, zooming slowly into a close-up, of Cary staring through the frosted window-panes of her home on the scene outside. Giving up Ron, Cary's isolation is complete. She can only watch and not participate in this fantasy. This short scene fades into the arrival of Kay and Ned for Christmas. The Scott residence is an image of affluent abundance, dominated by an enormous Christmas tree. Presents are exchanged and Ned leaves the room to prepare his mother's gift. This leaves time for Kay to announce her engagement to her mother. In the scene Kay is dressed in a red dress, echoing that worn by Cary at the start of the film, with connotations of Christmas, romantic passion and love. Kay's dress is contrasted with her mother's sombre black widow's outfit, speckled at the shoulders with diamante detail, resembling both snow and, perhaps more tellingly, tears. The exchange between Kay and Cary is shot in medium close-up. As Kay's romantic dreams are realised the look on Cary's face and the irony of the vase of red roses in the background, tells the audience that she realises her own dreams have been crushed. Cary's hopes are dashed further when Ned reveals that he will also be leaving and that the time has come to sell the family home. Cary's act of self-sacrifice in order to preserve her family has amounted to nothing, a sentiment that she articulates to her daughter: 'Don't you see, Kay? It's all been so pointless.'

The scene is then set for Ned to present his mother with her Christmas gift, which in the cruellest twist of fate is a television set. The 'last refuge of the lonely woman' that Cary had previously rejected is now presented to her as a substitute for a real life. As the television is wheeled into the room, the camera tracks round and pulls in close on Cary's distraught face caught in the reflective surface of the screen. The emblematic nature of this sequence has been referred to many times previously, its power is such that, as Fred Camper suggests:

> In an instant, in one of the most chilling moments in any film, we
> have a complete representation of the movement of the film as a

FIGURE 9 Cary isolated in her bourgeois home at Christmas in *All That Heaven Allows*

FIGURE 10 Cary, trapped in the reflection of the television screen, in *All That Heaven Allows*

> whole, the attempts of the other characters to reduce the appar-
> ently more real feelings she has for Ron Kirby to 'drama ... comedy
> ... life's parade at your fingertips'. The film, taken as whole, can
> almost be said to pivot around this single shot. The expressive
> force of every image, the meaning of every surface, is to some
> extent informed by its presence and implications. (1971: 54)

The gardener, Ron Kirby, offers an alternative to Cary's lonely and isolated
existence. Ron's iconography, attitude and milieux are set up in contrast to
the convention and conservatism of Cary's home and social life. From the
opening scene of the film Ron is symbolically linked to a typically clichéd
notion of nature. He is first seen outside tending Cary's trees, dressed in
warm, earthy-coloured clothes in contrast to the sombre suit worn by Cary
and the artificiality of Sara's appearance. As Thomas Schatz observes:

> Sirk's colour-coding of wardrobe indicates how material objects
> can become laden with thematic significance. This cumulative
> strategy develops along with the narrative and eventually provides
> as much information as the words and actions of the principal
> characters. (1981: 250)

In their opening conversation Ron is presented as enigmatic and distant,
not caring for the niceties of the polite conversation that Cary tries to

engage him in. Ron is the archetypical example of Sirk's 'immovable' character, in contrast to the constantly vacillating and uncertain Cary.

Later in the film Cary is introduced to Ron's friends Mick and Alida who have rejected the rat race and live a more 'natural' simple existence. Mick and Alida throw an impromptu party for Cary, inviting their disparate selection of bohemian friends. The revellers, Cary and Ron are seen dancing merrily, though we are reminded that Cary's introduction into this carefree world will be the cause of problems later, as during their festivities we notice, through a window in Mick and Alida's home, a fierce storm is gathering outside. In this scene Sirk makes an explicit link with Ron's 'natural' way of life and the Classical Liberal principles upon which American society was originally based. Cary notices that Mick is reading Thoreau's *Walden*, a nineteenth-century book dealing with the author's retreat from 'civilised' American society that is imbued with a strong social conscience and a passionate belief in individualism epitomised by the famous maxim, 'If a man does not keep pace with his companions, perhaps it is because he hears a different drummer. Let him step to the music which he hears, however measured or far away.' After reading this, Cary asks Alida if this book is Ron's bible (as it is Mick's); Alida tells her that Ron *lives* this ideal. Ron's lifestyle then is indicated as exemplifying an American ideal that has perhaps been lost and is certainly not evident in Cary's social circle.

Though it is hard for a contemporary audience to comprehend the ways in which *All That Heaven Allows* would have been read by its original intended audience it certainly seems that, as Schatz notes, 'the alternative "lifestyle" shown in *All That Heaven Allows* is scarcely a radical departure from the one that Cary has known' (1981: 251). Mick and Alida, irrespective of their surroundings, are still a conventional married couple, with Alida occupying a domesticated role. Ron, though a younger man, and seemingly free thinking, still adopts a paternalistic attitude towards Cary, forcing her to choose between the life and security that she has known or his 'new' way of living. Cary as widow, wife and mother, is the person who is expected to compromise and make sacrifices. As Alida tells Cary, Ron is absolutely not prepared to compromise. The only real alternative that Ron seems to offer Cary is symbolised by the home that he is building at the old mill. Rather than the cold tomb-like interior of the Scott residence, Ron offers Cary a modishly appointed barn conversion with a huge picture window overlooking a panoramic landscape.

The famous Christmas scene discussed earlier seems to be a point of temporary narrative resolution, though with Cary isolated and separated from Ron, a far from satisfactory one as it precludes the possibility of a happy ending. In order to achieve a satisfactory conclusion in such seemingly hopeless situations it is necessary to introduce a sequence of events governed by fate and chance rather than the, rather more 'logical', conventions of cause and effect. It is at this point that the film recourses to the *deus ex machina*. Cary visits her doctor complaining of persistent headaches. The doctor, an authority figure frequently positioned as the voice of reason in 1950s melodrama, suggests that Cary's headaches are physical manifestations of stress and that she should reconsider her decision to break up with Ron. Cary decides that the doctor is right and drives to the old mill to speak with Ron. When she arrives he is not at home and she leaves. Ron is in fact hunting with Mick and sees Cary's car from a rocky outcrop. He waves frantically to attract her attention but fails, in the process losing his balance and falling from a cliff, leaving him gravely injured in the snow. Later, Alida tells Cary of Ron's accident and she rushes to his bedside spending a sleepless night waiting for him to awake in the beautiful home he has made for her. When Ron does wake, it is to a snowy scene of picturesque beauty and artifice, seen from the picture window of the mill, and to Cary telling him, 'I've come home.'

A rapid and improbable sequence of events finally unites the couple with Cary seemingly forgetting the previously insurmountable obstacles of social convention and class differences that had separated them. The very fact of this speedy *volte-face* on Cary's part calls the 'happy ending' of the film into question but this resolution is made yet more problematic by the nature of their final union. As both Laura Mulvey (1977/78) and Jackie Byars (1991) have suggested, the ending, with Ron incapacitated and Cary nursing him, suggests not the happy union of the couple but Cary returning to a more socially acceptable role as 'mother' to Ron. As Mulvey notes:

> How can a mother of grown children overcome the taboo against her continued sexual activity in 'civilised society', when the object of her desire is reduced to child-like dependence on her ministrations? (1987: 79)

The influence of Sirk

Many film directors have cited Sirk and his distinctive cinematic style as an influence, from Martin Scorcese and Jonathan Demme to John Waters and Pedro Almodovar (discussed in the final chapter). However, the director whose work has been most closely linked to that of Douglas Sirk and whose style is most clearly informed by it is that of the German filmmaker Rainer Werner Fassbinder. Already an avant-garde theatre director with a film to his name, *Love is Colder Than Death* (1969), Fassbinder saw a retrospective of Sirk's films screened in Berlin and was reputedly so inspired by Sirk's techniques that he drove to Switzerland to speak with the retired director who was to eventually inspire the style and direction that Fassbinder's cinema would take for the rest of his short but prolific career. Combining Sirk's stylistic language with his own experience in experimental theatre Fassbinder would create a distinctive filmic language drawing together Sirkian, Brechtian and Artaudian devices.

Fassbinder was born in provincial Germany into a middle-class family and raised by his mother following her divorce from her husband (a doctor). It is interesting, and not a little ironic, that Fassbinder was brought up in a bourgeois household given his later involvement in political activism and the avant-garde theatre and film work he was to eventually become associated with. There are many parallels between the lives of Sirk and Fassbinder. Like Sirk, Fassbinder was to start his career in the theatre. In Munich in 1967 he joined *Action Theatre* where he was to meet many of the actors that would regularly appear in his later work in film. Jane Shattuc summarises the approach adopted by the *Action Theatre* collective:

> This leftist group was communally controlled by approximately seven members. The group adapted canonical works such as *Antigone*, *Leonce and Lena* and *Iphigenile*, investigating their intrinsic value by brazenly substituting for their themes the contemporary German political issues of the 1960s. (1995: 64)

Following Fassbinder's increasing involvement, *Action Theatre* was reorganised under his control as *Anti-Theatre* in 1968. *Anti-Theatre* was identified by the company as socialist theatre and Fassbinder's theatre work, from 1967 to 1974, was inspired and informed by the Marxist political activism of the 1960s and 1970s. This political dimension to his artistic endeavours was to continue to be important throughout his career. In short, Fassbinder was a politically motivated film director.

In 1969 Fassbinder made his first film *Love is Colder Than Death*, inspired by both the French New Wave (and in particular the work of Jean-Luc Godard) and the gangster films of Classical Hollywood. However, following his encounter with Sirk, Fassbinder's cinematic direction was to change and it is at this point that his mature and distinctive film style began to emerge. Fassbinder was extremely prolific, making 41 films in total over a relatively short period of just over ten years. During this period of frenetic activity, Fassbinder became a notorious figure in the German media due to his unconventional personal life and was recognised internationally as one of the key directors of the so-called 'New German Cinema'. The majority of textual analyses of Fassbinder's films highlights the connections between the director's techniques and the distanciation devices deployed by Brecht. As Shattuc observes:

Fassbinder's films share Brecht's interest in politics and form. In fact, many of them have strong affinities with Brecht's working-class subject matter and his alienating performance style. (1995: 87)

Though there is consistent evidence for these claims it was a connection that Fassbinder himself was to repeatedly refute. As Shattuc later notes Fassbinder's alienation techniques are stylistic rather than intellectual. It is perhaps more accurate to see Fassbinder's use of distancing devices emerging out of the inspiration and adoption of Sirk's techniques, which we have also noted have been related to Brecht. Fassbinder's work, like Sirk's, demonstrates *traces* of Brechtian techniques rather than a clear and direct relation to them. In fact, as an avant-garde director of the late 1960s, Fassbinder's style is perhaps even more clearly inspired by the techniques of Antonin Artaud, another hugely influential dramatist of the early twentieth century. Like Brecht, Artaud rejected the idea of a realistic theatre in favour of an extremely stylised and mannered form that he called the *Theatre of Cruelty*. Unlike Brecht however, Artaud was interested in exploring psychological states rather than questioning social order. In his *The Theatre of Cruelty: First Manifesto*, written in the mid-1930s, Artaud called for a radical new form of theatre that would 'arouse universal attention' (2001: 68). For Artaud, 'There can be no spectacle without an element of cruelty as the basis of every show' (2001: 77). Artaud lays out the form that this theatre would take, encompassing everything from subject matter to staging, costumes, theatre space and most importantly performance, which in his estimation should contain 'shouts, groans, apparitions, surprise, dramatic moments of all kinds' (2001: 72). Fassbinder's interest in Artaud was clear from his early days with *Action-Theatre* and this influence is not only evident in the stylised performances of his actors but made explicit at certain points in his films, as Shattuc points out:

The film *Satansbraten* (1975–76) begins with a quotation from Artaud's *The Theatre and its Double*. *Despair* (1977) is dedicated to 'Artaud, Vincent Van Gogh, Unica Zurn'. And in 1981, the year before his death, he wrote and directed a film, *Theater in a Trance*, that combined dance pieces with Artaud's writings. (1995: 96)

From 1971 onwards, Fassbinder's films demonstrate the drawing together of disparate influences: Hollywood cinema, Douglas Sirk, Brecht and Artaud. He was to frequently use a repertory company of actors, first encountered during his involvement with *Action Theatre*. Most notably the actress Hanna Schygulla would become something of a muse and appear in many of his films. Like several of Sirk's Hollywood melodramas, many of Fassbinder's films are concerned with the predicaments of female characters, frequently making huge demands on the ability to convey dramatic intensity in his actors, who, reputedly, he often treated notoriously badly.

Fassbinder used stylistic devices borrowed directly from Sirk in almost all of his films. The Sirkian use of vivid colour, for example, is echoed in *The Marriage of Eva Braun* (1979) and *Lola* (1981), a revision of Von Sternberg's *The Blue Angel*. The symbolic use of on-screen distance is deployed in *The Bitter Tears of Petra Von Kant* (1971) and *Fear Eats the Soul* (1973). Sirk's use of reflections and frames within frames is also very evident in *The Bitter Tears of Petra Von Kant* though the most excessive example of the use of reflections is found in *Chinese Roulette* (1976), seemingly set in a hall of mirrors. Sirk's love of elaborate and stylised *mise-en-scène* and anti-naturalistic lighting is also evident in *Querelle* (1982).

Following a technique favoured by Brecht and originally borrowed from the nineteenth-century tradition of theatrical melodrama, Fassbinder creates static visual compositions that act as momentary pauses in the action to illustrate the power relations and social and emotional rifts between characters. In *Fear Eats the Soul* this is illustrated by the scene in which Emmi first enters the Moroccan bar. Sitting alone at a table, her isolation is emphasised by the extended length of the narrow bar and the positions of the other patrons, seen in long-shot, seemingly miles away from her. Similarly in *The Bitter Tears of Petra Von Kant*, Petra's psychological collapse is visually conveyed at her birthday party where her guests stand in huddled compositions whilst she crawls around on the floor in a state of hysteria.

In many of Fassbinder's films the actors perform in a highly stylised and self-conscious manner, drawing attention to the very process of performance. This method, favoured by both Brecht and Artaud, is very apparent in *The Bitter Tears of Petra Von Kant* in which Margit Carstensen's performance imitates the mannered theatricality of classical Hollywood performance, a style of acting that would, today, be regarded as 'melodramatic' in a pejorative sense.

Referencing Artaud more specifically, Fassbinder encourages an even more stylised method in his last film, *Querelle*, in which the actors deliver their lines in a monotonous, ritualistic, fashion, as if they were being read. This effect is emphasised by his use of post-production dubbing, distancing the actor's voices from their performances yet further. Whilst this method of delivery is almost the exact opposite of melodramatic, declamatory performance, through the use of gestural actions and movement the effect achieved is not dissimilar to the highly theatrical manner of silent film performance.

Fassbinder also uses narrative and rhetorical techniques that can often have a disruptive effect. Most notably his films are stripped of the artifice of the happy ending so evident in Sirk's melodramas. In *The Bitter Tears of Petra Von Kant* for example, Petra is left alone at the end of the film. Trying finally to show some kindness to Marlene, the maid who has been a silent witness to the disintegration of her relationship with Karin and to whom she has shown nothing but contempt and cruelty, she is finally rejected. Marlene packs her bag at the prospect of their relationship being more equal and leaves Petra alone in the darkness. Fassbinder's films often end rather abruptly, precluding the possibility of a satisfactory conclusion, leaving the audience and the film's characters in an uncertain state of limbo. In *The Merchant of Four Seasons* (1971) for example, the protagonist, Hans Epp, dies, leaving his wife a widow. His death, however, is not presented as a tragic moment but rather as the inevitable and convenient conclusion to the life of a 'worthless' man. In the final scene his wife agrees to move in with Hans' best friend and the film seems to end almost in the middle of this highly significant and revelatory conversation. In *Querelle*, Fassbinder takes this disruptive approach still further: Lysianne's angry outburst in the bar of *La Feria* literally halts the narrative progression of the film in freeze-frame.

Fear Eats the Soul

Fear Eats the Soul is perhaps Fassbinder's most direct reference to the Sirkian melodrama. It is not (as has often been suggested) a remake of *All That Heaven Allows*, though it does make use of the same narrative

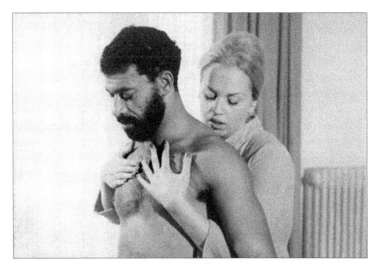

FIGURE 11 Emotional pressures lead Ali to infidelity in *Fear Eats the Soul*

formula of a relationship between an older woman and a younger man. In Fassbinder's film though, the older woman is not a wealthy bourgeois widow but an elderly, working-class cleaner, Emmi Kurowski (Brigitte Mira). Her lover-to-be is not a non-conformist gardener, but a black Moroccan labourer (played by Fassbinder's lover El Hedi ben Salem) whose noble Arabic name is shortened to 'Ali' by those around him.

At the start of the film Emmi goes for a drink in a local Moroccan bar where she meets Ali who tells her that he has to share a small apartment with a group of other immigrant workers. The kindly and widowed Emmi invites Ali to stay with her instead and they eventually become lovers. To begin with Emmi is unquestionably proud of her handsome and strong young boyfriend but increasingly becomes conscious of the prejudicial attitudes of those around her, including her work colleagues, neighbours, shopkeepers and her own relatives, who she financially supports with her lowly cleaning job. This prejudice is demonstrated, in Sirkian fashion, through dramatic compositions and confrontations that illustrate the increasing strains placed on the relationship between the naïve Emmi and Ali. Fassbinder undercuts the overt elements of social criticism with Sirkian irony. In a notable scene, Emmi takes Ali for a meal at Hitler's favourite restaurant, the *Osteria Italiana*. Emmi is seemingly entirely oblivious to the irony of choosing the Nazi leader's favourite restaurant as a venue for the celebration of her marriage to a black migrant worker. The couple sit, viewed in long-shot through a constricting doorway, in total isolation in the austere environment, whilst a waiter eyes them with silent distaste. The film ends, like Sirk's, with the romantic lead incapacitated, though this does not (as in the case of *All That Heaven Allows*) provide the opportunity for a happy resolution. Ali is diagnosed with a perforated stomach ulcer, which we are told is a perpetual hazard for immigrant workers. Added to this we discover that the complaint will recur after six months as immigrant workers are not entitled to the period of convalescence that they would need to fully recover. Hearing this catastrophic news, Emmi sits with the unconscious Ali, their reflections captured in a mirror, and cries at the hopelessness of his condition.

Todd Haynes: Far From Heaven

Whilst Fassbinder was renowned for utilising the stylistic techniques of Douglas Sirk there are other examples of filmmakers who have chosen not just to imitate the techniques but also to create contemporary recreations of the 1950s period melodrama. French director Francois Ozon for example, in *8 Women* (2002), freely adapts George Cukor's *The Women* transforming it into a melodramatic thriller with the lavish cinematic spectacle of a Technicolor 1950s melodrama. Todd Haynes' *Far From Heaven* is another interesting example of an attempt to update the Sirkian melodrama for a contemporary audience. Earlier in his career Haynes had already engaged with melodrama's preoccupation with the stifled existence of the bourgeois housewife in his second feature, *Safe* (1995). Set in contemporary California, *Safe* recounts the story of affluent homemaker Carol White (Julianne Moore) who unexpectedly develops allergies to her environment that become so extreme that she is ultimately forced to leave her family home and relocate to a sanctuary in the desert. Filmed primarily in detached long shots the film's ironic critique of New Age philosophy and the shallow and empty quality of bourgeois life is evocative of Fassbinder's approach to such material. With his later film, *Far From Heaven* (2002) (also starring Julianne Moore), Haynes was to reference Sirk's style far more explicitly. The title of Haynes' film clearly indicates its source material (*All That Heaven Allows*) whilst simultaneously making the ambiguity of Sirk's original film title rather more literal; from the outset the audience understands that this film is located in a world that is far from perfect. Unlike Sirk's contemporary reception, Haynes' film has received almost unanimously positive reviews and both the film's script, cinematography, Elmer Bernstein's score and Julianne Moore's performance have received Academy Award nominations, indicating not just the skilled realisation of a now anachronistic filmic style but also the extent to which the status of the once reviled Hollywood melodramas of Douglas Sirk and his contemporaries has changed over time. Though in Haynes' own estimation, the melodrama is still 'perhaps the most degraded form of narrative experience you can pick for a contemporary audience', it is now clearly regarded as a legitimate vehicle for social critique. The film has been described in popular reviews as a 'post-modern' melodrama, working as a meticulous exercise in style, creating a painstaking facsimile of the aesthetic patterns of a 1950s film. Haynes himself is partly responsible for the 'post-modern' tag applied to the film through his identification in interviews of elements of self-reflexivity in the excessive style of the 1950s melodrama. In production notes appearing in the film's website he observes,

> While the look and style of those 1950s melodramas is anything but realistic, there's something almost spookily accurate about the emotional truths of those films. They are hypereal, that's why we call them melodramas. (www.farfromheavenmovie.com/index2.html)

Whilst *Far From Heaven* most clearly references *All That Heaven Allows*, like Fassbinder's *Fear Eats the Soul*, it is not a remake but rather takes the narrative outline of Sirk's film, conflating themes from *Imitation of Life* and *Written on the Wind*, into a film that echoes, rather than imitates, the originals. Additionally, *Far From Heaven* deals with themes that would have been impossible for the 1950s melodrama to countenance for both societal reasons and also due to the stipulations of the production code. Homosexuality, for example, a forbidden subject in 1950s Hollywood, is presented as the reason for the problems that lie beneath the superficially successful marriage of the Whitakers. Sirk himself noted that it came to his attention after filming was complete that his film *Interlude* was, in fact, a Hollywood rewrite of a James Cain story, *Serenade*, dealing with homosexuality:

> I did not know that *Serenade* was behind it at all. I only found out afterwards that Universal had owned *Serenade* for years, and that the Stahl picture, too, had been based on it. If conditions had been

different, and especially if I had a different script based on the original James Cain novel, I think that it could have been a terrific picture – at least a very unusual one. The original James Cain story is a cruel story, partly set in Mexico – and, of course, it is about homosexuality. All that had to go, and in the process the story lost its bite. (1987: 127/8)

Similarly both Vincente Minnelli's *Tea and Sympathy* (1956) and William Wyler's *The Children's Hour* (1961) had to be extensively altered in order to make their themes of homosexuality and lesbianism respectively, acceptable.

Cary Scott's widowhood in *All That Heaven Allows* is transformed in Haynes' film into Cathy Whitaker's loveless marriage, her oppression and isolation is turned in on itself even more maliciously than in Sirk's film through the dilemma of carrying the burden of a secret (her husband's homosexuality) that it is genuinely impossible for her to share with anyone.

The romantic alternative to Cathy's loveless life in *Far From Heaven* is, as in the case of *All That Heaven Allows*, presented by her gardener. Here, however, it is not merely the problems of class and age difference that are barriers to the couple's romance but also the rather more inflammatory question of race; Raymond Deagan is black. Once more Haynes introduces a narrative device – the potential of interracial relationships – that for some sections of an American audience might still be regarded as politically loaded but would have been completely inconceivable within the constraints of 1950s Hollywood cinema. Haynes further complicates the possibility of romance between the couple by presenting societal pressures as exerted not exclusively by white racism but from within the black community itself where Cathy is treated with similar hostility and suspicion that she receives from her friends. Whilst *Far From Heaven* lacks the systematic stylistic techniques that are so marked in Sirk's films, carefully coded *mise-en-scène* is still used, creating environments that fill in the absences created by what cannot be said or demonstrated by characters. In a notable scene, Cathy visits her daughter at a ballet recital. Cathy asks her daughter where her friends are, and she points to the back of the venue where a group of mothers and daughters are grouped in a brightly-lit back room, silently staring at Cathy and her daughter who appear isolated in the darkened auditorium. The rhetoric of this sequence, dramatically emphasising Cathy's rejection by her community represented through on-screen distance, and the use of the frozen tableaux of the mothers and daughters echoes the stylistic techniques used by both Sirk and Fassbinder.

The work of Fassbinder and Haynes illustrates that melodrama continues to exist outside of 1950s Hollywood cinema and also the ways in which the stylistic techniques, originally attributed to Douglas Sirk, have been appropriated and developed by a generation of filmmakers informed by debates around melodrama within film criticism. The work of these directors also begins to demonstrate the need for a more encompassing and progressive theoretical framework in which to understand melodrama in cinema, an approach that is not constrained within the confines of the 'family melodrama', nor by auteurist debates, genre theory, Neo-Marxist ideological critiques or feminist concerns about the 'women's film'. What is needed is an approach that can build upon the body of literature that has emerged concerning melodrama in cinema and additionally acknowledges the ways in which melodrama can manifest itself across genres and connects with audiences through rhetorical techniques designed to elicit emotion and empathy. This third way of thinking about melodrama, as a sensibility rather than as a genre or style, will be explored in the final chapter.

3 SENSIBILITY

Beyond genre

> Critics and historians of moving images have often been blind to
> the forest of melodrama because of their attention to the trees of
> genre. (Williams 1998: 61)

Melodrama consists of much more than the Hollywood family melodrama
and the 'woman's film'. Since the 1980s, some film scholars have been
rethinking melodrama beyond generic boundaries, as a style, mode,
sensibility, aesthetic and rhetoric, crossing a range of genres, media,
historical periods and cultures. During the mid-to-late 1980s, film scholars
began to turn attention away from investigations into the ideology of the
'family melodrama' and the 'woman's film' to find ways of understanding
the distinctive narrational and aesthetic effects of melodrama across a
diversity of genres, sub-genres and film cycles. High on the agenda was
melodrama's use of pathos and its emotional impact on audiences. So too
was melodrama's relationship to realism. Increasingly, film melodrama
was linked to stage and literary melodrama, establishing it as part of a
much wider tradition. At the same time, the term 'melodrama' was applied
to an expanded (and expanding) canon of films. Instrumental in this shift
of direction for film scholarship on melodrama was the influence of Peter
Brooks' *The Melodramatic Imagination: Balzac, Henry James, Melodrama,
and the Mode of Excess* (originally published in 1976 and reprinted in
1985). This book has played a major role in the re-conception of melodrama
within Film Studies. It has, amongst other things, provoked a return to the

issue of melodrama's historical development on stage and screen. It has also made pathos one of the defining features of melodrama. On both counts, this has redirected film scholarship on melodrama back towards the debate initiated by Thomas Elsaesser in his seminal 1972 study, 'Tales of Sound and Fury'.

Melodrama as a mode

In 1986, inspired by Brooks' *The Melodramatic Imagination*, Christine Gledhill began the process of reorienting the debate on film melodrama towards a more sustained investigation of the operations of pathos. Her contribution to a dialogue (with E. Ann Kaplan) on 'Stella Dallas and Feminist Film Theory' established the new terms for understanding melodrama as a distinctive mode. Working with the notion of three modes – realism, melodrama and modernism – Gledhill drew upon Brooks' thesis on melodrama in order to conceive it as 'an aesthetic and epistemological mode distinct from (if related to) realism, having different purposes, and deploying different strategies, modes of address, and forms of engagement and identification' (1986: 45). Where realism ignores and modernism exposes gaps in bourgeois ideology, melodrama insists on the realities of life in bourgeois democracy and, at the same time, implicitly recognises the limits (inadequacies) of conventional representation (for example, exposing the limits of language, its inability to express or articulate certain contradictions). In this way, the 'beneath' or 'behind' (the unthinkable or repressed) is evoked as metaphor through gesture, music and *mise-en-scène*. In Gledhill's account, melodrama was a mode altogether distinct from the classic realist text.[1] She argued that only when film scholars embraced this fact would the debate successfully move on from an ironic and dispassionate appraisal of melodrama's excesses and absurdities to a more authentic assessment. This would entail understanding how melodrama was meaningful when taken at face value, in all seriousness: how, for instance, it was able to move audiences to tears.

Gledhill also noted that the rhetoric of film melodrama was still an 'uncharted field' (ibid.). Only Thomas Elsaesser, she claimed, had provided an account of melodramatic rhetoric in the cinema up until the mid-1980s. Gledhill was particularly interested in his analysis of pathos and, in her own short essay, embarked upon a brief but perceptive discussion of how pathos functions in melodrama. Most crucially, she drew attention to an essential paradox of the form. Although melodrama is primarily concerned with an intense focus on interior personal life, its characters (including the central protagonist) are not psychologically constructed and, rather than being introspective, convey their inner being through action, movement, gesture, décor, lighting and editing (1986: 46). This results in the spectator possessing knowledge that is not available to the characters themselves and this discrepancy contributes directly to the operation of pathos: 'Pathos involves us in assessing suffering in terms of our privileged knowledge of its nature and causes' (ibid.). This is an application of Brooks' point about melodrama's play with the revelation of the protagonist's virtue, which is misunderstood due to 'misleading appearances, fatal coincidences, missed meetings, etc., all of which lead to a misrecognition of that character's nature or intent' (1986: 46). In this account of melodramatic rhetoric, pathos emerges as an 'aesthetic activity' (1986: 47). This, moreover, is 'intensified by the misrecognition of a sympathetic protagonist because the audience has privileged knowledge of the "true" situation' (ibid.).

Melodrama and pathos

The importance of pathos within melodrama and its operation through point of view and knowledge (between characters and between audience and characters) emerged even more strongly in 1986 in Steve Neale's essay, 'Melodrama and Tears'. As the title suggests, Neale was explicitly concerned with the way in which 'tear-jerking' constitutes a key component of melodrama's effect upon audiences and why audiences find the process of crying pleasurable and satisfying. He begins his essay by talking about melodrama as a 'mode of narration' and examines the specific ways in which melodrama orders and motivates its narrative events. Melodramas are defined here largely by the specific kinds of narratives they employ. For instance, 'melodramas are marked by chance happenings, coincidences, missed meetings, sudden conversions, last-minute rescues and revelations, *deus ex machina* endings' (1986: 6). They also involve continual surprises and sensational developments. Neale suggests that such narratives are essentially unrealistic in the sense that 'the succession and course of events is unmotivated (or under motivated) from a realist point of view' (ibid.). He claims that such preparation and motivation that does exist is always insufficient and that the tendency is towards excess over cause, extraordinary over ordinary (for example, fate, chance and destiny).

For Neale, the key to the narrative logic of melodrama is not realism or naturalism but rather the need to produce discrepancies between the knowledge and point of view of the spectator and the knowledge and point of view of the characters. This discrepancy is ultimately what produces the pathos that culminates in tears. Timing plays a crucial role here. Pathos results, Neale explained, from a realisation (characters discovering what the spectator already knows) that comes too late or almost too late (that is, just in the nick of time): 'tears come whether the coincidence comes too late or just in time, provided there is a delay and possibility, therefore, that it may come too late' (1986: 11). Throughout the period of delay (whilst the spectator waits to see if the characters will discover what they already know), the spectator is unable to intervene, to change the events or the misconceptions of the characters. Tears result, in part, from this power-lessness. Moreover, the longer the delay (the longer the spectator feels this powerlessness) the greater the emotional impact on the spectator when the moment of realisation arrives.

The dramatic expansion of the melodramatic field

Recognition of the basic narrative structures of melodrama and the pin-pointing of the mechanisms by which it provokes tears from its specta-tors, constituted an important first step towards rethinking melodrama beyond the limits of specific and easily-identifiable generic categories and film cycles. This shift in critical thinking about melodrama was even more marked a year later when the first published anthology of studies on film melodrama and the 'woman's film' was published under the title of *Home is Where the Heart Is*. Here, in Gledhill's introductory chapter, 'The Melodramatic Field: An Investigation', a radically new conception of melodrama was set out and a new methodology for studying melodrama was proposed. Written just three years after she had outlined the form as a genre in her section on melodrama in *The Cinema Book* (Cook 1984), Gledhill now outlined the development of melodrama criticism in Film Studies and found it wanting. She noted the largely pejorative use of the term 'melodrama' by film scholars, which had prevailed in film criticism until Douglas Sirk's 1950s films had been rehabilitated, regarded as ironic and subversive critiques of American ideology. Prior to this, she claimed, melodrama had been used by critics as the 'anti-value for a critical field in which tragedy and realism became cornerstones of "high" cultural value' (1987: 5). For such critics, melodrama not only lacked the seriousness and intellectual weight of either tragedy or realism but, perhaps more importantly, was associated with mass entertainment (that is, with its appeal to the lowest common denominator). The rise of genre criticism in the 1960s concentrated on discrete and readily demarcated cinematic categories like the western and gangster film. In contrast, melodrama seemed too messy and uncontainable (as fragmented across genres and pervading others such as the western and gangster film), lacking a clear evolution on screen and being thematically inconsistent. Gledhill noted, however, that radical shifts within Film Studies reversed this situation, bringing melodrama to the fore.

In the late 1960s and early 1970s, realism (for example, the 'classic realist text') was increasingly seen as a reactionary form, bound up with bourgeois values. Ideological analysis provided a new critical context in which melodrama emerged 'with full force into this reconstituted critical field' (1987: 6). The advent of Neo-Marxist film theory in the 1970s created a new context for examining (and celebrating) stylistic excess and narrative inconsistency, these attributes prized for their abilities to expose ideological contradiction. As we have explained in the previous two chapters, Sirk's 1950s films played a leading role in this respect; his style and his ironic stance heavily informed notions of melodramatic conventions in Hollywood cinema. As Gledhill put it, 'there occurred a slippage of the "subversion" argument from its attachment to Sirk as "author" to melodrama itself' (1987: 7). She pointed out that Sirk's authorial signature was now expanded to a generic trademark, the genre of the Hollywood family melodrama constructed out of the 1950s films of directors such as Minnelli, Ray, Ophüls, Cukor and Kazan. Gledhill saw this as the expansion of the parameters for a new critical field. At this point, scholars began to wonder what kind of field melodrama offered (genre, style, mode, ideology, and so on).

Reviewing the early film scholarship on melodrama, Gledhill suggested in 1987 that the most useful work was Elsaesser's essay 'Tales of Sound and Fury'. This was partly because it included a historical review of film melodrama's theatrical and literary antecedence and partly because it recognised melodrama as the basis of Hollywood's aesthetic, emotional and cognitive effects. Another important and valuable feature of Elsaesser's piece, for Gledhill, was that it recognised and gave due consideration to the importance of pathos. Of course, what most film scholars in the 1970s and 1980s found valuable about Elsaesser's essay was that it offered the possibility of conceiving of melodrama as a coherent genre;

namely, the 'Hollywood family melodrama of the 1950s'. This provided a much more straight-forward way of thinking about and investigating melodrama than if one were to take the form as an aesthetic or mode which pervaded Hollywood across virtually every decade and every genre, sub-genre and film cycle.

By 1987, Gledhill had come to regret that in the late 1970s and early 1980s 'the issue of melodrama as a formative cinematic mode was not pursued' (1987: 8). She pointed out that this would have entailed a wholesale re-conceptualisation of the form and entailed extensive investigation, particularly into the relationship between realism and melodrama. But in the new critical climate of 1970s' film criticism, realism (not melodrama) was the anti-value and 'realist' texts, under the umbrella of the 'classic realist text' (whether films, novels or television programmes), were condemned as inherently reactionary since they reproduced bourgeois and/or patriarchal ideology. Gledhill argued that the construction of melodrama as the family melodrama, as a specific Hollywood genre, 'made it difficult to pursue its connections with the nineteenth-century melodramatic traditions which ... constituted a founding tradition of Hollywood as a whole' (1987: 12). She challenged this approach by questioning (or demanding a justification) for the confinement of melodrama to films about domestic situations and 'feminine' conditions, suggesting that the themes of the western are just as excessive. She asked, 'if melodramatic rhetoric informs westerns, gangster and horror films, psychological thrillers and family melodramas alike, how tenable is it to constitute melodrama in a critical, disruptive relation to the classic realist/narrative text?' (1987: 13). Gledhill was now describing not a specific group of films that could be labelled 'melodrama' but, rather, a 'melodramatic rhetoric' that a range of films of different genres could utilise. To understand the rhetoric of melodrama, Gledhill perceived that first of all film scholars would have to stop thinking of melodrama and realism as inevitable opposites or as mutually exclusive categories. Consequently, she called for a much more systematic and thorough-going exploration of the relationship between the two modes.

In her introductory chapter to *Home is Where the Heart Is*, Gledhill offered an example of a more wide-ranging cultural and aesthetic investigation. In the sections headed 'Historicising Melodrama' (1987: 14–28) and 'Melodrama as a Cultural Form' (1987: 28–38), she examined the historical relationship between melodrama and the bourgeoisie, drawing upon Brooks' *The Melodramatic Imagination* of 1976. In the process, she also examined the performative and aesthetic traditions of stage melodrama and the narrative traditions of stage and literary melodramas. This also involved the institutional and political factors that shaped the aesthetics and rhetorical devices of melodrama as a theatrical form.

The undertaking of such a potentially large academic project within the limited space of a chapter was (it would appear) to fill a perceived gap within Film Studies, undertaking the type of work which could have logically followed on from Elsaesser's essay in 1972 had the ideological debate not imposed itself. Confined as it was to two sections of an introductory essay to the anthology of critical studies on melodrama and the woman's film, Gledhill's project here could never have been more than a sketch or a provisional investigation. Its purpose was to instigate a new approach and a new area of investigation for scholars of film melodrama rather than provide the definitive account. What it did do was identify an alternative body of scholarship on melodrama that film scholars might usefully consult in order to understand its historical development, cultural significance and aesthetic aspects.

Much of Gledhill's revised notion of film melodrama has been derived from Brooks' study of melodramatic theatre and literature. More than any other single source, this book has been instrumental in the perception of melodrama as a mode. In opposition to the more pejorative and restrictive notion of melodrama that had emerged in Film Studies by the 1980s, Brooks perceived melodrama as a 'modern mode', that used the rhetoric of realism alongside an aesthetic of 'muteness' to make sense of everyday life in a modern and secular world. Brooks understood melodrama as a dramatic and literary form that developed in post-sacred cultures where society needed to find a secular system of ethics and of making everyday life meaningful in the absence of religion. He referred to this as the 'moral occult' and saw it as involving a psychic need as well as an ideological one (that is, the need to make sense of life for personal and social reasons). If theatrical forms are to articulate or represent such meanings and ethical values, they necessarily require a degree of realism. The issues, in other words, need to be made relevant to people's ordinary lives. Brooks' assertion that traditionally melodramas have fulfilled this function simultaneously insists that they also required a level of realism in order to win audience recognition and assent (rather than being opposed to realism). Whilst perceiving the necessity for melodramas to use realism as part of their aesthetic, Brooks also described them as being similarly determined by 'muteness' whereby speech was replaced by music, gesture and expressive *mise-en-scène* for dialogue, giving melodrama its distinctive form.

Melodrama and morality

Central to understanding the ideology of melodrama is its Manichean outlook: that is, its polarities of good and evil, vice and virtue, innocence and villainy (as black and white). For Brooks, melodrama always involves ethical conflicts, symbolically rendered (but never abstract). Initially, characters were emblematic (such as mother, father, son, daughter) and the drama was invariably built around the triadic relationships of a hero, heroine and villain, each being clearly, even elaborately, defined and distinguished. The opposition of vice and virtue, good and evil, innocent hero/heroine and villain, insists upon suffering and pathos. The good (hero and/or heroine) suffer as a direct consequence of their virtue, goodness and innocence, falling prey to the evil vices of the villain. Pathos is evoked for the audience and the other characters who witness the suffering of the virtuous innocents, culminating in almost excruciating moments of sympathy and pity at the sight of such prolonged and undeserved suffering. This constitutes the ultimate melodramatic scenario and the ultimate melodramatic emotion and becomes, for Gledhill, what film melodrama is really all about whatever specific form it takes (historical costume romance, science fiction, crime thriller, horror or western adventure):

> Characteristically the melodramatic plot turns on an initial, often deliberately engineered, misrecognition of the innocence of a central protagonist. By definition the innocent cannot use powers available to the villain; following the dictates of their nature, they must become victims, a position legitimated by a range of devices which rationalise their apparent inaction in their own behalf. Narrative is then progressed through a struggle for clear moral identification of where guilt and innocence really lie. (1987: 30)

This was a critical statement, describing in precise terms the rhetoric of melodrama that would transform its conception within Film Studies as a mode: as, indeed, the pervasive mode of American cinema. This rhetoric also enables us to see, as Geldhill notes, Steven Speilberg's adaptation of *The Color Purple* (1984) directly linked to D. W. Griffith's *Way Down East* (1920), both having victimised innocent heroines persecuted wrongfully by their husband/lover, both films driven to identify good and evil.

Melodrama emerged from Gledhill's introductory chapter to *Home is Where the Heart Is* as something far more wide-ranging and pervasive than anything described in the other studies of melodrama and the women's film included in that anthology (i.e. the established critical literature). Here it was recognised as a cross-class and cross-cultural form, of mixed heritage, both bourgeois and popular. It was dominated by a non-verbal aesthetic (spectacle, gestural performances and music) but had undergone a series of aesthetic transformations involving fantasy and realism as well as spectacle. It was an intertextual form which drew (promiscuously) on journalism, legitimate theatre, opera, paintings, poetry, songs and popular fiction, for inspiration and adaptation.

Melodrama and realism

Gedhill's essay 'The Melodramatic Field' charts melodrama's history, from European (chiefly France and England in late eighteenth century) to American theatre, to the birth of cinema and its development from silent to sound pictures. What is stressed throughout is the interdependence of melodrama and realism in this development. Realism, is recognised here not as a static form but rather as one that has to consistently change as social and cultural perceptions of truth change. Gledhill sees realism as opening up new areas for representation which, once uncovered, melodrama assumes. Moreover, realism's relentless search for renewed truth and authentication pushes it towards stylistic innovation, whereas melodrama's search is for something lost, producing a more nostalgic attitude that can accommodate not just established forms of representation but even archaic ones. Melodrama's attachment to an outmoded past has frequently resulted in its derision.

Melodrama is neither realism nor its opposite. For Gledhill, it takes 'its stand in the material world of everyday reality and lived experience, and acknowledging the limitations of the conventions of language and representation, it proceeds to force into aesthetic presence identity, value and plenitude of meaning' (1987: 33). Whereas realism seeks to possess the world by understanding, melodrama seeks to 'force meaning and identity from the inadequacies of language' (ibid.). This approach to understanding melodrama enabled the re-evaluation of the relationship of melodrama and the woman's film as proposed within Film Studies. Gledhill further noted that the identification of melodrama with the woman's film had been a 'retrospective categorisation' that was a consequence of realism's association with masculinity (ibid.) and how historically the realm of feeling has been assigned to women whilst realism has become associated with masculine restraint, hence the cultural prohibitions on men weeping in public:

> Very soon cinema was constituted as an inherently 'realist' medium and it has become a given of film history that while early cinema produced melodrama by default, the power of speech instituted a critical break between a cinema destined for realism and its melodramatic origins. At the same time genre divisions were consolidated, allowing melodrama a separate identity ... which facilitated critical boundaries drawn by gender. The 'classic' genres were constructed by recourse to masculine cultural values – gangster as 'tragic hero'; the 'epic' of the West; 'adult' realism – while 'melodrama' was acknowledged only in those denigrated reaches of the juvenile and the popular, the feminised spheres of the woman's weepie, the romance or family melodrama. (1987: 34)

Gledhill asserted, however, that many of Hollywood's classic genres retained their melodramatic pre-dispositions and noted that 'the industry recognised this pervasive melodramatic base in its exhibition categories – western melodrama, crime melodrama, sex melodrama, backwoods melodrama, romantic melodrama and so on' (1987: 35). Indeed, she noted a fundamental paradox here, that it was actually the male genres of westerns and gangster films and other action genres that perpetuated a melodramatic rhetoric. Meanwhile, the woman's film (later to be described as melodrama by scholars) adopted quite a different form, being dominated by words and dialogue, openly expressing and articulating its central issues and conflicts. Such films were, in other words, anything but texts of muteness, forced to transform the unspeakable into spectacular action sequences or *mise-en-scène*. Nevertheless, it was the male genres that took on the aura of prestige associated with realism, whilst women's genres became increasingly linked with the pejorative associations of melodrama.

Revising the Film Studies' account of melodrama

Gledhill's position was almost entirely at odds with the other studies contained in her anthology (although sharing occasional sympathies). It was, in many ways, a call for the adoption of a completely new approach to melodrama within Film Studies rather than an endorsement of the approaches that had been taken already. Her position has subsequently been taken up most enthusiastically and most explicitly by Linda Williams. In her essay, 'Melodrama Revised', she offered a 'revised theory of a melodramatic mode – rather than the more familiar notion of the melodramatic genre' (1998: 43). She argued that melodrama, rather than being a genre or any other sub-set of American filmmaking, is *the* pervasive American mode of filmmaking, constituting many genres and being ever-present.

Melodrama is the fundamental mode of popular American moving pictures. It is not a specific genre like the western or horror film; it is not a 'deviation' of the classic realist narrative; it cannot be located primarily in women's films, 'weepies' or family melodramas – though it includes them. Rather, melodrama is a peculiarly democratic and American form that seeks dramatic revelation of moral and irrational truths through a dialectic of pathos and action. It is the foundation of the classical Hollywood movie. (1998: 42)

Williams' arguments and observations were largely informed by Brooks' *The Melodramatic Imagination* and Gledhill's work on melodrama, adopting the thesis that melodrama has been the means of articulating vice and virtue in a post-sacred world. She argued that melodrama is ultimately concerned with articulating moral values and establishing moral right, which usually involves a central protagonist whose moral virtue goes unrecognised by other characters in the film (but, crucially, not by the audience) until the climax of the narrative. Throughout her essay, Williams argued that as melodrama has developed on the American screen it has modernised itself and, effectively, disguised itself by adopting tropes of 'realism' and developing more fully realised characters. She urged film scholars to look beyond these to recognise the more fundamentally melodramatic nature of American movies (old and new): 'If emotional and moral registers are so sounded, if a work invites us to feel sympathy for the virtues of beset victims; if the narrative trajectory is ultimately more concerned with a retrieval and staging of innocence than with the psychological causes of motives and actions, the operative mode is melodrama' (ibid.).

Williams' project was to re-inscribe the melodramatic mode into the history of American cinema, arguing that it lingered on throughout the sound era in many genres (including action movies). For her, the term 'melodrama' indicates a form of exciting, sensational and, above all, moving story. Constructing a new history of American film melodrama, she linked together American forms such as the novelistic romances of Nathaniel Hawthorne, Harriet Beecher Stowe and Mark Twain, the popular theatre of Belasco, Aitken and Boucicault, the silent films of Griffith, DeMille and Borzage and the sound films of Ford, Coppola and Spielberg. The common thread uniting them is, for Williams, 'the combined function of realism, sentiment, spectacle and action in effecting the recognition of a hidden or misunderstood virtue' (1998: 54).

Williams chooses American Vietnam films, including *The Green Berets* (1968), *The Deer Hunter* (1978), *Rambo* (1982), *Platoon* (1986) and *Casualties of War* (1989) to make a striking case for the pervasive nature of melodrama. These most male-oriented of action movies might at one time have seemed the very antithesis of Film Studies' definition of melodrama as family melodramas and women's films. Good reason then for Williams to claim that 'what makes them tick is … not simply their action-adventure exploits but the activation of such exploits with a melodramatic mode struggling to "solve" the overwhelming moral burden of having been the "bad guys" in a lost war' (1998: 61).

Moreover, 'what counts in melodrama is the feeling of righteousness, achieved through the sufferings of the innocent' (ibid.). Williams warned that neither the realism nor the virility of action should fool us into thinking that action films are not melodramas. This is a way of opening out the 'genre' of melodrama. Williams makes what she herself admits is a 'bold statement' which is that, rather than a submerged, embedded tendency within realist narrative, melodrama has been the dominant form of popular cinema. She argued that as melodrama has developed it has shed its old-fashioned values, acting styles and ideologies along the way whilst continuing to deliver the melodramatic experience. Consequently, the structures and effects of American cinema are in essence melodramatic. Hence, Williams claims:

> the basic vernacular of American moving pictures consists of a story that generates sympathy for a hero who is also a victim and that leads to a climax that permits the audience, and usually other characters, to recognise that character's moral value. The climax revealing the moral good of the victim can tend in one of two directions: either it can consist of paroxysm of pathos (as in the woman's films or family melodrama variants) or it can take that paroxysm and channel it into the more virile and action-centered

variants of rescue, chase, and fight (as in the western and all the action genres). (1998: 58)

This strategy makes all Hollywood cinema, except for comedy, melodramatic given that the revelation of moral superiority is such a central and recurrent feature of American filmmaking.

Facing up to the tears

'In cinema the mode of melodrama defines a broad category of moving pictures that move us to pathos for protagonists beset by forces more powerful than they and who are perceived as victims' (Williams 1998: 42). This broad definition of melodrama does not simply classify all films that make audiences cry 'melodrama' (because some films that can make audiences cry are not melodrama). It does, however, recognise the importance of the affective and emotive power of film melodrama to move audiences to tears.

In reviewing the Film Studies' account of melodrama from the 1970s and 1980s, Williams noted that the 'so-excessive-as-to-be ironic model rendered taboo the most crucial element of the study of melodrama: its capacity to generate emotion in audiences' (1998: 44). She pointed out that whilst Geoffrey Nowell-Smith suggested that emotion was syphoned off into the *mise-en-scène*, he said nothing about the emotional reactions of audiences. Williams claimed that the 1970s criticism of melodrama implied two different forms: 'bad' melodrama of manipulated, naively felt, feminine emotions and 'good' melodrama of ironical hysterical excess thought to be immune to the more pathetic emotions (ibid.). She also noted that feminist film scholars were just as silent on the topic of emotion as their male counterparts. In the early to mid-1980s, feminists regarded the 'quintessentially feminine emotion of pathos' as a key aspect of women's oppression (whereas anger meant liberation). Tears of pity or (even worse) self-pity would not help women in their bid to transcend patriarchal power and control. Williams noted that in her own writings from this time she too refused to acknowledge the importance of melodramatic pathos, choosing to argue that images of female pathos could engender anger on the part of female spectators:

Both drawn to and repelled by the spectacle of virtuous and pathetic suffering, feminist critics were torn: we wanted to properly condemn the abjection of suffering womanhood, yet in the most loving detail of our growing analyses of melodramatic subgenres ... it was clear that something more than condemnation was taking place. (1987: 47)

She further wrote that, 'in the process of distinguishing our "properly" feminist distance from melodrama's emotions, we failed to confront the importance of pathos itself and the fact that a surprising power lay in identifying with victimhood' (ibid.). Williams added that the feminist critics of the woman's film (herself included) were 'convinced that pathos was, in itself, an excess of feeling that threatened to overwhelm the emerging liberated woman' (1998: 48). Yet she claimed that underlying much of the feminist work on the woman's films in the 1980s was the implicit but unspoken question of what it meant for a woman viewer to cry at the end of a film. Here she also hinted at another unspoken assumption: men do not cry at movies. Interestingly, however, she refuted this claim by noting that male action films 'pivot upon melodramatic moments of masculine pathos' (ibid.). In such moments, heroic failure often leads to what Thomas Schatz had referred to in conversation with Williams as a good 'guy-cry'. The fact that this reference to male tears was confined to a footnote suggests some hesitancy in tackling the subject. Similarly, the fact that there is no attempt to authenticate the claim beyond this instance of anecdotal evidence (that is, based on spoken rather than written testimony) also suggests that in the late 1990s the topic of male crying was virtually taboo in Film Studies. However, within the main body of her essay, Williams did return to the issue of male tears. She wrote that 'strong emotions that can move audiences to tears are not the special province of women, but of the melodramatic "feminisation" that ... has been a persistent feature of American popular culture at least since the mid-nineteenth century' (ibid.). If men crying at movies is considered in these terms ('feminisation') it is no wonder that they are not prepared to admit to it and that film scholars are so hard-pressed to find tangible evidence of male crying as a regular feature of melodrama. The question of whether male and female viewers cry at the same things in a melodramatic film has barely arisen within film scholarship, constituting another uncharted area.

A large section of Williams' essay is devoted to an analysis of D. W. Griffiths' *Way Down East* and much of this analysis is given over to the role of pathos, to the function and provocation of tears. Indeed, she used the film to illustrate that

A melodrama does not have to contain multiple scenes of pathetic death to function melodramatically. What counts is the feeling of loss suffused throughout the form. Audiences may weep or not weep, but the sense of loss that implicates readers or audiences is central. (1998: 70)

Her discussion of pathos drew on Steve Neale's earlier work, adapting and revising his ideas and observations. Whilst noting Neale's argument that we cry due to the fulfilment of our own infantile fantasy (crying being a demand for satisfaction and our tears sustaining that fantasy), Williams disagreed with his view of crying as the product of powerlessness. She argued instead that in melodrama tears may be a source of future power because they acknowledge the hope that desire will be fulfilled. Williams interpreted them as almost an investment in the future and not just a longing for what has passed and cannot be regained (1998: 71). Even she acknowledged, however, that we need a better understanding of the role played by tears in melodrama, specifically in terms of how it is orchestrated by the temporal and rhythmic elements of melodramatic rhetoric. Film scholars also need, as Williams has suggested, a better appreciation of the teasing delay and forward-moving march of time of melodrama, its stop-go progress and the role this plays in provoking tears. What we might add to this is how this process works differently, if at all, for different types of audience (for example, male and female).

It is clear from Williams' discussion of crying at the movies that, even by 1998, much more detailed and wide-ranging research was still required within Film Studies. Her account certainly marked an advance in this direction. Just simply recognising that, in melodrama, the spectator seldom cries at the end simply because the character cries, moved beyond one of the existing basic assumptions. She argued that film scholars needed to give greater consideration to the 'complex negotiation between emotions and emotion and thought' (1998: 49). Furthermore, Williams states that 'the idea that each character in melodrama sounds a single emotional note that is in turn simply mimicked by the viewer – has impeded the serious study of how complexly we can be "moved"' (ibid.).

Pathos and action

Williams attempted a much more sophisticated understanding of emotion in melodrama than in previous accounts. She argued, for instance, that pathos is always in tension with other emotions in melodramas and also that it is directly related to the action, often the most compelling, dramatic, spectacular and memorable action of a film. Later in her essay, Williams described at length how the pathos of Lilian Gish in Griffiths' *Way Down East* provokes the final climactic action of the film, its most famous sequence involving a death-defying rescue on a moving ice-floe.

Following Peter Brooks' line of argument, Williams asserted that a 'quest for a hidden moral legibility is crucial to melodrama' (1998: 52). This often results in big sensation scenes that present moral truths (often in gesture). These are never fully spoken in words, they constitute the 'unspeakable truth'. Revelation occurs as spectacular moving sensation (usually as gesture accompanied by music) sustained through physical action without dialogue. Thus, Williams wrote that, 'Melodramatic dénouement is typically some version of this public or private recognition of virtue prolonged in the frozen tableau whose picture speaks more powerfully than words' (ibid.).

Throughout her essay Williams emphasised the relationship between pathos and action in melodrama, distinguishing melodramas by their high quotient of pathos *and* action. She explained the importance of this aspect of melodrama by citing Brooks' thesis:

> If, as Peter Brooks argues, melodrama is most centrally about moral legibility and the assigning of guilt and innocence in a post-sacred, post-Enlightenment world where moral and religious certainties have been erased, then pathos and action are the two most important means to the achievement of moral legibility. (1998: 59)

The revised model of film melodrama

Williams has stated that 'film criticism may do well to shift from the often myopic approach to the superficial coherence of given genres and toward the deeper coherence of melodrama' (1998: 62). In the course of conducting her case study of Griffiths' *Way Down East* she identified five melodramatic features central to American cinema:

i)   melodramas begin and end in a space of innocence. Lost innocence provokes nostalgia that in turn provokes pathos

ii) melodramas focus on victim-heroes and the eventual recognition of their virtue

iii) melodramas employ an aesthetics of astonishment: at the point where virtue is at last recognised there is a prolongation of emotional effect that often sets up the need for action (the climactic action)

iv) melodramas employ a dialectic of pathos and action, establishing a tension between being 'too late' and 'just in the nick of time'; time is the ultimate object of loss, this loss provoking tears

v) characters in melodrama embody primary psychic roles organised in Manichaen conflicts of good and evil. Melodramatic characters are monopathic: that is, lacking more complex mixes of feelings and psychological depth.[2]

These five distinct features of melodrama (as a mode) are to be found across a wide range of genres, sub-genres and film cycles. Such a model enables a seemingly diverse group of films to be compared, such as westerns (for example, *Stagecoach* (John Ford, 1939)), fantasy adventures (*The Thief of Bagdad* (Michael Powell, 1940)) and heritage cinema (*Maurice* (James Ivory, 1987)). Irrespective of generic differences (in theme and style), what makes films correspond to this model is the fact that they provoke tears and that their narratives develop by concealing and eventually revealing a character's moral virtue or innocence. To examine such films in relation to this model involves exploring the way in which the audience's knowledge and point of view are established in opposition to that of the leading characters, enabling the audience to anticipate misconceptions, false assumptions and injustices regarding the victim-protagonist. It also involves recognising the extent to which their characters are essentially lacking in psychological depth and emotional complexity, that they are set in direct opposition to other characters, creating a polarisation of attitudes, desires and goals. This is a particular way of seeing the world, a particular way of representing themes and characters and organising the audience's knowledge and sympathy with these. What is melodramatic about these films is not that they deal with a set of specific themes, have certain kinds of characters or use a specific iconography but rather that they reveal a particular approach whatever the themes being dealt with and whatever types of characters are involved. It is the expression of a certain kind of sensibility, requiring audiences to adopt a melodramatic sensibility in order to understand, appreciate and enjoy these films, in order to be able to go with the flow (for example, to be prepared to let the tears flow).

A melodramatic sensibility

The more fluid and progressive conception of melodrama as a mode, argued for by Christine Gledhill and others, is a significant development in discussion around the subject and has wider implications for the study of melodrama and the melodramatic as an expressive code or sensibility in cinema. As Gledhill persuasively argues, considering melodrama as a mode rather than as either a genre or a style has significant benefits:

> The notion of modality, like register in socio-linguistics, defines a specific mode of aesthetic articulation adaptable across a range of genres, across decades and across national cultures. (2000: 229)

Regarding melodrama as a mode thus facilitates the consideration of the ways in which a melodramatic sensibility can manifest itself across a range of texts and genres. Thinking of melodrama in these terms is rather more liberating than the predetermined Film Studies accounts that Gledhill notes has 'relegated melodrama as outmoded' (2000: 235). It creates the possibility to discuss forms of expression and representation that are ephemeral or fragmentary; scenes in films that are excessive and yet have an emotional power or resonance, for example. It also enables scholars in film, literature, theatre and art history to re-evaluate the value-laden binary oppositions between realism and melodrama. Gledhill indicates that this reconsideration of melodrama in opposition to realism is already taking place:

> There is now underway a vigorous debate between theatre and film scholars around the 'baton' model of stage-screen relations whereby it is supposed the practices of the popular nineteenth-century theatre are passed over to cinema, cleansed of their melodramatic trappings and made fit for the twentieth century, thus installing another boundary between 'old-fashioned' structures of moral feeling and contemporary demands for realist perception. (2000: 231)

Peter Brooks' work on theatrical and literary melodrama, for example, argues that a melodramatic sensibility manifests itself across theatrical and literary texts and is in fact a singularly modern rather than an 'old-fashioned' mode of expression. One has only to look at the pioneering examples of realist theatre such as Ibsen's *A Doll's House* and *Hedda Gabler* or Strindberg's *Miss Julie* to see that melodramatic situations are repeatedly used in plays that scandalised contemporary audiences due to what was regarded as their frank subject matter and 'realistic' portrayal of contemporary life. To modern audiences by contrast, Nora dancing the tarantella in a desperate bid to distract her husband in *A Doll's House*, Hedda throwing Lovborg's manuscript in the fire and finally committing suicide in *Hedda Gabler*, and the almost ritualistic portrayal of the master/servant relationship in *Miss Julie* are not dissimilar, in either register or treatment, to the conflicts, tensions and hysterical climaxes of the Hollywood family melodramas of the 1950s.

Regarding melodrama as a modality also makes it possible to consider a range of films produced outside of the mainstream of Hollywood film production and consider the extent to which melodramatic aesthetics and techniques are deployed to convey emotional conflicts. Popular Hindi cinema, colloquially known as 'Bollywood' cinema, for example, is especially receptive to readings that demonstrate a melodramatic sensibility in operation. Ravi Vasudevan (1989) draws on Peter Brooks' account of melodrama to analyse Indian cinema. In films such as Kamal Amrohi's *Pakeezah* (1971), a story of courtesans, star-crossed lovers, history repeating itself, improbable coincidences and mistaken identities, the dramatic tropes, excessive spectacle substituting for words and clear sense of a moral order that Brooks identifies as features of theatrical melodrama are very apparent. For example, in an especially notable scene, the film's protagonist, condemned to life as an ostracised courtesan, dances on shattered glass at the wedding of her lover. This hysterically dramatic sequence acts as the catalyst for the revelation of Pakeezah's (a name meaning 'pure of heart') true identity to be revealed and a satisfactory conclusion to the film whereby the heroine is freed of the shame of her current existence and reunited with her lover in marriage. Of equal interest, both Nick Browne and Ma Ning (1994) have discussed the social and political significance of melodrama as a mode of expression in the cinema of the People's Republic of China. It is not just popular cinematic forms like Bollywood (which very evidently draws directly on the strategies of theatrical melodrama) and Chinese cinema that demonstrate the manifestations of a melodramatic sensibility, however. The work of Ingmar Bergman for example, usually categorised outside of the mainstream of popular cinema as 'art house', frequently deals with thematic concerns and demonstrates a stylistic aesthetic that might be understood as articulating a melodramatic sensibility. Films like *Persona* (1966) with its theme of muteness, or the claustrophobic atmosphere evoked in *Cries and Whispers* (1972), both featuring female protagonists, are especially good examples of the ways in which Bergman's cinema could be read as melodrama.

Equally the films of the Dogme 95 movement such as *Festen* (Thomas Vinterberg, 1998) and, especially, *Breaking the Waves* (1996), *The Idiots* (1998) and *Dancer in the Dark* (2000) (all directed by Lars von Trier) whilst utilising a scrupulously realist aesthetic, deal with highly-charged emotional states and situations, seemingly pushing the boundaries of realism to its limits in ways that can provoke extreme discomfort in audiences. Once again this cycle of films that challenge audience expectations and have the ability to elicit strong emotional responses through their charged dramatic register are prime examples of the melodramatic sensibility at work in contemporary cinema outside of the Hollywood mainstream. Yet there is a potential danger here in assuming that all forms of emotion and sentiment are conveyed in an intrinsically melodramatic fashion. There is therefore the need to be mindful that melodrama engages with and manifests itself through extremes of emotion and is a rhetorical strategy that struggles to convey charged emotional and psychic states through visual and dramatic means. Melodrama, in this way, exists at the very limits of a visual and dramatic medium like cinema; it attempts to articulate those things that it is almost impossible to represent – melodrama speaks the unspeakable and represents the unrepresentable. Much of the scholarly work into the ways in which a melodramatic sensibility inflects cinema outside of Hollywood is yet to be done but this small sample of examples indicates some of the interesting directions that these investigations may take in future.

Consideration of melodrama as a mode or sensibility, then, broadens the parameters of what constitutes melodrama and the ways in which the term can be usefully applied in the first instance. The other important development that this more progressive understanding of the term enables is to break the longstanding and problematic link that has prevailed in Film Studies between melodrama and the 'woman's film'. As Gledhill points out:

> Inevitably, given the weak twentieth-century commonsense boundary between anything labelled 'woman's' and melodrama, the woman's film and melodrama are frequently (but not invariably) treated by critics – both journalistic and academic – as one. (2000: 225)

Though it is important to acknowledge that important developments in the understanding of melodrama in cinema have been brought about as a direct consequence of this linkage and the crucial intervention of Feminist film scholars, the possibility of discussing melodrama and its effects in operation outside of films aimed at a female audience creates conditions in which it is possible to discuss a much wider sample of filmic texts and genres. In particular genres more generally associated with male audiences either through theme or mode of address come into view as demonstrating a melodramatic sensibility.

The male melodrama

The category of male melodrama, as Gledhill implies, already exists within the standard Film Studies account of the family melodrama, though it is usually seen as a diversion from the, more usual, female centred melodramas of 1950s Hollywood. Laura Mulvey points to the differences in narrative strategies between melodramas with a male protagonist which, she argues, tend to result in the resolution of 'irreconcilable social and sexual dilemmas' (1977/78: 56) and films with a female protagonist where resolution cannot be achieved. Thomas Schatz also identifies 'male weepies' as a distinct subdivision of the Hollywood family melodrama. He argues that such films as *Bigger Than Life*, *East of Eden*, *Rebel Without a Cause* and *The Cobweb* deal with the problems of 1950s masculinity and the need for the male protagonist to assume, in some form or other, the role of patriarch within a family unit.

For Schatz, in these films, concerned with two character types – the archetypical, aging father and inadequate son – 'the central conflict involves passing the role of middle-American "Dad" from one generation to the next' (1981: 239). The 'male weepie' cycle, of course, has continued to the present day and can still be regarded as a type of cinema in which the assumption of a paternal role is discussed in emotionally charged terms. *Dead Poet's Society* (Peter Weir, 1989) for example, dealing with the inspirational English professor John Keating, is notable for its tear-jerking qualities and extremely emotional mode of address. Mike Hammond notes the parallels, as well as the significant shifts that have taken place, between the 1950s and the 1980s construction of this particular form of melodrama:

> Where the 1950s melodrama had to chart a path between arbitrary and formal resolution of conflicts and letting the 'crises of

identification follow their self-destructive course' the 1980s male melodrama ... dispenses with the latter and, instead of questioning the power of authority, it reinforces it through the production of all-male families and by investing in the masculine the reproductive powers of the feminine. (1993: 60)

Phil Alden Robinson's *Field of Dreams* (1989) even more clearly falls within the parameters of the standard Film Studies account of the male melodrama. The film deals with the story of Ray Kinsella, an Iowan farmer who begins to hear voices in his dreams that tell him to create a baseball field on his farming land. Kinsella is presented as an idealised American family man, clearly linked to the countries' agrarian, pioneering heritage. Ray is in possession of a dream that no one else shares or understands, a dream that symbolically represents the American dream of individualism and personal freedom. This dream threatens the stability of Ray's home-life and his livelihood as a farmer and, towards the end of the film, his farm is on the verge of repossession through the intervention of a duplicitous in-law and the concerns of bankers representing the heartless bureaucracies of corporate America. The film's resolution is especially notable for its emotional and affective qualities with the dream of the baseball field realised and the magical appearance of sporting figures from America's past as well as the apparition of Ray's own, long dead, father. Through its highly emotive narrative and rhetoric the film suggests the potential, even if only through fantasy, of regaining the liberal ideals of what is presented as a lost America and the possibility of reconciliation with the past through the pursuit of dreams.

The melodramatic sensibility and the action movie

Moving outside of the Film Studies designation of the family melodrama as a generic category it is possible to see a melodramatic sensibility in operation in a wider range of male-orientated texts and genres. Nowhere is this truer than in the genre of the action movie, frequently concerned with staging conflicts between polarised moral forces (good vs. evil). Action movies inevitably, though frequently inadvertently, explore gender constructions and primarily the construction of masculinity itself, either to assert, and thereby celebrate, masculinist values, or in some cases, to call them into question. The excessive, spectacular and overstated nature of the action movie, especially those of the 1980s, lends itself particularly well to a discussion of the ways in which melodrama manifests itself outside of the terrain of the family melodrama. By investigating the action movie as an articulation of the melodramatic sensibility it is possible to salvage and apply several of the conceptual models proposed by scholars who have discussed the generic category of the 'family melodrama'. In this way, by thinking about melodrama as a sensibility, we are able to build upon, rather than merely dismiss, the substantial body of academic work undertaken into the connections between melodrama and cinema that has been discussed in the previous two chapters.

Two films made in the 1980s by John McTiernan, a director who specialises in action movies, demonstrate very clearly how melodramatic rhetorical and narrative techniques are frequently deployed in action movies more generally.

Die Hard

A hugely popular film that established television actor Bruce Willis' credentials in cinema and has resulted in two sequels with a third to be released in 2005, *Die Hard* (1988) can be regarded as a melodrama in the classic theatrical sense and also as a melodrama according to Steve Neale's 'historicist' account of the term based on industrial categorisation. As we noted in the first chapter Neale argues that, for the film industry at least, melodrama 'meant crime, guns and violence; they meant heroines in peril; they meant action, tension and suspense; and they meant villains' (2000: 179). This description of melodrama as concerned with spectacular action and suspense epitomises the concerns and affects that *Die Hard* engages with. The film also conforms to Peter Brooks' identification of the sensibility that expresses itself in theatrical melodrama in the eighteenth and nineteenth centuries. *Die Hard*, like the classical theatrical melodrama, concerns the virtuous but lowly hero (the policeman, John McClane) who finds himself inadvertently tested through, what Brooks describes as 'the introduction of menace or obstacle, which places virtue in a situation of extreme peril' (1976: 31). *Die Hard* is, to use Brooks' words, a 'text of muteness' in which gesture and, in the case of this particular film, spectacular action substitutes for words. McClane, we understand from the outset of the film, is overworked and often away from home. His professional commitments as a New York law enforcer have inevitably had a negative impact on his family life, meaning that he is becoming increasingly estranged from both his children and Holly, his wife. Holly also has a pressurised job within the corporate world and has relocated, with her children, to Los

Angeles. McClane struggles to combine the patriarchal role of father with that of bread-winner and the film suggests that his failure in this respect, as well as his wife's rejection of the role of home-maker and the implicit suggestion that she rejects his status as patriarch (it is revealed that she uses her maiden name at work) threatens the stability of their home. This context provides the narrative backdrop for the dramatic and spectacular assertion of McClane's masculinity.

McClane arrives at his wife's place of work, the Nakatomi Plaza, on Christmas Eve to confront his wife and unsuccessfully resolve their differences. Through remarkable circumstance, at the same time, a group of European terrorists enter the building, taking everyone, including Holly, hostage. Just as John McClane personifies the heroic American everyman, so the terrorists, led by Hans Gruber (Alan Rickman), are clearly codified through their sophisticated uniform of dark European tailoring and their Germanic accents, as the personification of evil. As Brooks observes of the villain of the classical melodrama:

> He is reduced to a few summary traits that signal his position, just as physically, do his swarthy complexion, moustache, cape, and concealed dagger. But he is strongly characterised, a forceful representation of villainy ... The villainy at issue may be more or less motivated ... And in almost every case it appears somewhat

FIGURE 12 The melodramatic villain Hans Gruber holds Holly captive in *Die Hard*

inadequate to the quantity of villainy unleashed. The villain is simply the conveyor of evil, he is inhabited by evil. (1976: 33)

McClane, alone in his wife's office is left undetected by the terrorists and the stage is set for the classical Manichean conflict between good and evil enabling McClane to perform his narrative function as hero. Through a succession of daring escapades, including explosions, leaping from burning buildings and crawling barefoot over broken glass, all designed as extreme trials of his determination, the heroic and virtuous McClane is finally able to save the hostages and his wife, simultaneously preserving his marriage and ultimately reasserting his patriarchal status.

Predator
If *Die Hard* conforms in many ways to the tropes of theatrical melodrama, epitomising a melodramatic sensibility and aesthetic concerned with the moral conflict between the forces of good and evil, then McTiernan's earlier film, *Predator* (1987), starring Arnold Schwarzenegger, can also be regarded as demonstrating a melodramatic sensibility, through its problematic representation of the signs of masculinity as spectacle and its hysterical attempts to counter alternative or oppositional readings. Susan Jeffords (1994) argues that the emergence of the muscular action hero of the 1980s coincides with the right-wing conservatism of the Reagan administration and an anti-feminist backlash with the attempt to reassert patriarchal ideals through culture. Films such as *Rambo* (George Cosmatos, 1985) and those starring Schwarzenegger, in particular, *Conan the Destroyer* (Richard Fleischer, 1984), *Conan the Barbarian* (John Milius, 1982), *Commando* (Mark L. Lester, 1985), *The Running Man* (Paul Michael Glaser, 1987), *Red Heat* (Walter Hill, 1988) and *Total Recall* (Paul Verhoeven, 1990) as well as Jean Claude Van Damme in *Kick Boxer* (Mark Di Salle, 1989) and *Double Impact* (Sheldon Lettich, 1991), though in some cases made after the Reagan administration ended in 1989, illustrate this tendency well. This is not to say that popular cinema simply reproduces dominant ideology but rather that the ideological agenda of any given historical period (and the debates and contradictions that lie within and beneath ideology) can be read, symptomatically, in cultural products including Hollywood cinema. *Predator* is an interesting case inasmuch as it vividly asserts a reactionary macho masculinity typical of the 1980s action movie whilst simultaneously through its recourse to a melodramatic mode of address and excessive, hysterical *mise-en-scène*, calls this ver-

sion of masculinity into question. By drawing on Geoffrey Nowell-Smith's work on 1950s melodrama, especially his argument concerning conversion hysteria and the return of the repressed, it is possible to identify *Predator* as manifesting a melodramatic sensibility.

In *Predator*, Dutch (Schwarzenegger) and his team of mercenary commandos are sent to the jungles of Central America on a secret mission to rescue American airmen captured by terrorists. Their mission fails, resulting only in the capture of a local woman and they soon find themselves trapped in the jungle. On their journey to a rescue point, the commandos are attacked by an unseen enemy who seems to take pleasure in the gory dismemberment of human (almost exclusively male) bodies. The commandos realise too late that they have become the prey of a mysterious non-human creature and it is left to Dutch, after the rest of his team have been killed, to finally confront the creature that has been attacking them. From the outset of the film Schwarzenegger's physicality is presented as spectacle. In a notable scene at the start of the film he is reunited with a colleague and greets him with a handshake that emphasises, in close-up, his overdeveloped biceps. The rapidly edited and exaggerated close-up is so emphatic in its assertion of Schwarzenegger's macho masculinity that it seems parodic. Once in the jungle, both Dutch and his colleagues, who are all uniformly muscular, are soon presented sweating and bare-chested in the exotic, sultry environment. The possibility for interpreting this, often gratuitous, display of all-male, spectacular, muscled masculinity as a homoerotic scenario within the context of a mainstream Hollywood action movie must, naturally, be disavowed at all costs. The potential for this reading is diminished in the first instance by the introduction of a superfluous female character and, earlier in the narrative through a scene where the commandos exchange crude sexual jokes. Irrespective of these attempts at recuperating heterosexual masculinity however, the film struggles to deny the potential for this reading throughout and recourses to a *mise-en-scène* that is hysterically excessive. The commandos' cache of weaponry, for example, is unfeasibly large, each of them possessing a gun that seems to outdo the previous one in its magnitude and potential for destruction. Their iconography as characters is similarly excessively coded as stridently macho, to such an extent in fact that it seems almost ironic. Unintentionally, the commandos do not so much function as epitomes of macho manhood, they seem rather more like 'The Village People' transplanted to the rain forest. The predator itself is equally problematic and again opens itself to the possibility of an oppositional reading.

FIGURE 13 The commandos demonstrate their firepower in *Predator*

Originally the predator is invisible, hidden both from the audience and the commandos. At this point, the creature watches the commandos from the safety of the jungle, detecting them by the heat of their bodies. When the creature is finally revealed its physicality is clearly masculine and dressed in what appears to be the futuristic, black-leather clad accoutrements of a biker with a head-dress of what appears to be dreadlocks. Through iconographical elements then he is presented as both racially and sexually 'othered'. This sense of otherness is emphasised by the revelation of the reasons for the predator's bloodthirsty pursuit of the commandos, which, it seems, is in order to make a gruesome necklace of human skulls that he wears as a trophy. The predator's actions seem motiveless and excessive in their violence. In *Predator* the creature is presented, through his racial and implicit sexual differences, as a threat to conventional patriarchal masculinity and it is only the true epitome of that particular version of masculinity, Dutch, who can defeat him and restore order. In this light, drawing on Nowell-Smith's arguments it is possible to see the melodramatic sensibility employed in *Predator* to reassert dominant ideas of masculinity even as it problematises them. The film, in effect, contains a subtext that deals with the heterosexual fear of homosexual contamination.

This reading then brings us to the final set of debates that this book will deal with; the connections between melodrama and a gay sensibility.

Melodrama and the gay sensibility

Whether regarded as a genre, a cinematic style, or as a mode/sensibility, melodrama has almost always been the subject of interest for film scholars because of the ways in which it opens up discussions around questions of gender and sexuality within cinematic texts. As we have seen throughout this book investigations into the ways in which discourses of femininity and the feminine are articulated in the woman's film for example, undertaken largely by feminist academics, have often focused debate on melodrama and its relationship to cinema aimed at a female audience. Likewise, the more recent developments in the study of the cultural construction of masculinity and the ways in which masculinity is represented and played out in cinema enable a much broader range of films to be identified as demonstrating melodramatic narrative and stylistic techniques and a melodramatic sensibility. From the mid-1980s onwards sexuality has become an increasingly significant area of debate in Film Studies. This is largely due to the intervention of gay and lesbian scholars working within the discipline and also to the development of gay and lesbian studies and queer theory as theoretical paradigms. With these developments within Film Studies as a discipline in mind, questions of gay spectatorship and a gay sensibility and their relationship to melodrama emerge. Whilst this is still a rather marginalised area of investigation it is nonetheless one interesting direction that discussion around melodrama may take in future.

Camp

It is notable that the films that have been collectively identified as melodramas through the standard Film Studies account have spoken to audiences other than the, largely assumed, female audience for the woman's film. The most conspicuous group who have found the 1950s family melodrama of particular interest are gay men. The gay male appreciation of these films, however, has usually been due to their spectacularly unintentional manifestations of camp. Camp is a difficult subject to summarise in a few sentences. As Barbara Klinger notes 'Cultural critics tend to define camp by discussing three of its aspects: camp taste, camp practitioners and camp politics' (1994: 134). Susan Sontag's essay, 'Notes on Camp', though dated, remains one of the most perceptive descriptions of what camp is and what camp does. Both scholars note that camp is a fundamentally subversive method for re-reading and creating cultural products, a reading strategy that takes pleasure in the excessive and the fake. As Sontag puts it, 'a good taste of bad taste' (1966: 291).

As both Klinger and Gledhill have noted Douglas Sirk's Universal melodramas had attracted a gay following as camp texts many years before they were 'recovered' as examples of subversive Hollywood cinema by Film Studies academics. Films like Sirk's, as well as examples from the oeuvres of Minnelli, Ray, Cukor, Wilder and Losey, achieved cult status within the gay subculture as a direct consequence of the very excessiveness, extreme emotionality, mannered performances, style and very direct sentimental form of address that these films demonstrate. In fact, many of the features that film theorists would later suggest were the basis for the family melodramas' canonical status as subversive, progressive texts were the very qualities that gay men identified as a source of humour. In a chapter dealing with camp reception of Sirk's films, Klinger provides several textual examples of the camp excesses of the Universal melodramas:

> Sirk's melodramas lend themselves to a kind of exposé of gender stereotypes. In *Imitation of Life* when Susy runs out on a balcony to proclaim to her mother and their party guests, 'Oh, Mama, look! A falling star!', or when Marylee responds to her brother's accusation that she is a filthy liar with 'I'm filthy, period', the roles of virginal and debauched women, respectively, reach the level of caricature. (1994: 151)

Klinger also notes that camp is often concerned with an ironic revision of the anachronisms of past attitudes or aesthetic devices:

> From the Victorian ethos surrounding an illegitimate birth in D. W. Griffith's *Way Down East* (1920) to the anti-marijuana hysterics of *Reefer Madness* (1936) to Dorothy Malone's nymphomania in Sirk's *Written on the Wind* (1957), what represents one era's supreme scandal can strike a future generation's funny bone. (1994: 143)

It is nonetheless ironic that gay audiences should take such pleasure in films that so repeatedly celebrate heterosexual union and so consistently deny the existence of gay desire at all. Jane Shattuc suggests that this is due to two factors:

Gays not only identified with the marginality of the melodramatic form as a 'castrated culture', they displaced their sexual identities onto the melodrama's heroine as a victim of patriarchal discourses on sexuality. (1995: 101)

So, for Shattuc at least, melodrama is not just the object of camp appreciation for gay men due to its excesses and outmoded representations of gender roles, it is also of interest to gay men because of its lowly status as a form of representation aimed (as is often argued) at women primarily and finally because the female heroines of such films provide a figure of identification for gay men, a group who are often denied any representation in cinema.

Klinger notes that whilst camp has traditionally been associated with the gay subculture, within a more media literate, contemporary culture, camp has become available as a reading strategy to a much wider audience. The pleasures of camp therefore are no longer confined to gay audiences but can be accessed by the general public. Klinger refers to this phenomenon as 'mass camp' epitomised by the fashion for parodic or ironically self-reflexive humour in television and cinema more generally. Camp however still has strong associations with gay men and gay culture and is perhaps the most evident expression of a gay sensibility just as melodrama, a dramatic mode that engages with intense emotional and dramatic conflict still attracts the interest of gay audiences and increasingly over the past thirty years has become a form of expression that has interested a generation of gay filmmakers in a variety of ways.

Gay cinema and the gay auteur

Gay cinema is far too broad a subject to summarise satisfactorily here, and a more detailed exploration of the social and cultural history and significances can be found in Richard Dyer's *Now You See It* (1990), which charts the emergence of gay and lesbian cinema in underground cinema and elsewhere. It is nonetheless true to say that the gay affinity with melodrama as an expressive code manifests itself in many examples of gay and lesbian cinema. From the theatricality and emotional crescendos of the cinematic adaptation of Harvey Fierstein's play *The Torchsong Trilogy* (1988), through a succession of films dealing with the shattering consequences of the AIDS crisis, such as *Longtime Companion* (Norman Rene, 1990) and *Savage Nights* (Cyril Collard, 1992), to the affecting, true-life story of Teena

Brandon, *Boys Don't Cry* (Kimberly Pierce, 1999), gay cinema frequently deals with crises, dilemmas and the effects of social prejudice and in order to address difficult or controversial themes has often recoursed to the rhetoric of melodrama.

There are also several examples of gay directors who have adopted the Film Studies designation of the family melodrama for their own uses. Rainer Werner Fassbinder and Todd Haynes, discussed in previous chapters, both openly gay and both leading figures in the New German Cinema and the New Queer Cinema respectively, have drawn on the Sirkian melodrama in the course of their careers. In Fassbinder's case, Sirkian techniques are used to create subversive critiques of attitudes towards a range of issues from racism, social prejudice, bourgeois ideology and contemporary German society and in Haynes' work to explore gay sexuality, New Age religion, and contemporary suburban America. The gay French filmmaker Francois Ozon has also used the stylistic devices of the Hollywood melodrama in *8 Women* (2001), the emotional address and distanciation devices of Sirk in *Under the Sand* (2000), as well as directing his own cinematic version of Fassbinder's play *Water Drops on Burning Rocks* (2000), dealing with the complexities and power dynamics in relationships both gay and straight.

An even more explicit example is offered by the work of John Waters. Famed for his low-budget cinema and deployment of a kitsch aesthetic, Waters' cinema is imbued with a vividly camp humour that over the years has been diluted to some degree to appeal to a wider mainstream audience. From the outset of his career in the late 1960s, Waters' films positioned themselves in an unusual narrative terrain, somewhere between the 1950s melodrama, social problem film and exploitation movie. The stylistic excesses, contrived narratives and hysterical performances of the melodrama, however, were a particular source of inspiration. In his early (and most notorious) films, Waters repeatedly used a small group of performers, often friends, and consistently cast the drag star, Divine, in a leading role, often playing the victimised heroine roles associated with the woman's film. In *Polyester* (1981) for example, Waters' directly references the Sirkian melodrama, combining narrative themes from both *All That Heaven Allows* and *Written on the Wind*. In the film, Divine plays Francine Fishpaw, a suburban housewife, trapped in a loveless marriage to a local pornographer with two delinquent children (a drug addict, foot fetishist son – the notorious Baltimore foot stomper – and a nymphomaniac daughter) and a money-crazed duplicitous mother. Francine bears the brunt of the communities' rage with her disreputable family. Francine falls in love with a younger man, Todd Tomorrow (played by 1950s star Tabb Hunter) who offers her the prospect of happiness and an escape from her stifling and miserable existence. Sadly Francine discovers, too late, that Todd is, in fact, a chancer, hired to steal the Fishpaw fortune and run away with her mother. In a further acknowledgement of the gimmicks of 1950s cinema, *Polyester* was originally screened with the distribution of scratch and sniff cards to be used at key moments in the film where Francine's highly attuned sense of smell is a key narrative device. Similarly, in *Female Trouble* (1975) Divine plays Dawn Davenport, a young woman who embarks on a life of crime as a direct consequence of her parents failing to provide her with her longed-for Christmas gift of a pair of cha-cha heels. The unfortunate Ms. Davenport eventually finds herself on death row, echoing the hysterical dénouement of the Susan Hayward vehicle *I Want to Live!* (Robert Wise, 1958). As Richard Dyer notes in his study of lesbian and gay cinema, it is through this reappropriation of the contrivances of 1950s melodrama that a gay sensibility emerges, often through camp parody and in some cases through explicit, though still comedic, expression:

> In *Female Trouble*, Edith Massey declares 'The world of the heterosexual is a sick and boring life' and it is just this that the films show, but with a gleeful sense of the gross that make them intoxicating. (1990: 170)

Perhaps the most prominent contemporary example of a gay director inspired by melodrama is to be found in the work of the Spanish film-maker Pedro Almodóvar. Almodóvar's early cinema, such as *Pepi, Luci, Bom and Other Girls on the Heap* (1980) or *The Labyrinth of Passion* (1982), was not dissimilar to the work of Waters inasmuch as the films were designed for shock value, featuring a repertory company of friends and with low production values. However, though Waters' cinema has remained resolutely low budget and outside of the mainstream, success has meant that Almodóvar's cinema has become increasingly sophisticated making full use of the potential of widescreen colour photography, elaborate production design, star performers – in fact, the full armoury of devices that Thomas Elsaesser has noted contributed to the expressive range of the 1950s melodrama. Almodóvar is a well-documented fan of the 1950s woman's film and this influence is very evident in his use of female protagonists who are, often, either mothers or middle-aged women.

FIGURE 14 Leo's mother and sister provide colic relief in *The Flower of My Secret*

These characters often appear to be points of identification for Almódovar himself. In *The Flower of My Secret* (1995) for example, Leo (Marissa Peredes) is a lonely author of romantic fiction who begins to realise that the romantic dreams that populate her successful novels are illusions. Throughout the film, material is included that points up the connection with Leo and Almodóvar himself. For example, Leo discards one of her manuscripts which is later sold to Bigas Lunas (another famed Spanish director) who we are told has developed it into a screenplay, a sly suggestion perhaps that material that Almodóvar would reject is the best that Lunas can hope for. Later in the film Leo returns with her mother to the small town of Extremedura, the town where we are told she was born and also Almodóvar's home town.

Like the cinema of Fassbinder and Waters, Almodóvar's films include relatively few gay characters, and the protagonists, with the exception of those in *The Law of Desire* (1987), are almost always heterosexual. The gay sensibility in his films is expressed through narrative twists and turns that confound our conventional expectations of heterosexual romance, the inclusion of characters whose sexuality is ambiguous or whose sexual identity or gender identities are in flux. There are many examples here; the transsexual Tina in *The Law of Desire*, the revelation that Manuela's lover, the father of her child is now a transsexual and Huma Rojo's lesbianism in *All About My Mother* (1999), the sadomasochistic relationship in *Tie Me Up, Tie Me Down* (1990), the sexual ambiguity of Benigno in *Talk to Her* (2002) and Angel in *Matador* (1985). The recurrence of these characters creates a sense of a world in which preconceptions of 'normal' sexual behaviour are constantly questioned and undermined.

The contemporary interest in the narrative and stylistic strategies of the films that the standard Film Studies account has designated as melodrama points to a final irony in discussion around melodrama as either a genre, style or sensibility; irony and paradox, of course, being characteristic of melodrama as a means of expression. Just as Film Studies academics have seemingly reached a point at which melodrama is no longer the focus of heated debate that it was in the 1970s and 1980s, and have seemingly also reached something of an impasse in terms of either establishing what melodrama is and what its function or significance is, so filmmakers, many of them emerging from film schools and academic backgrounds where they would have been introduced to many of the academic debates on the subject, have once again alighted on and found a renewed interest in the family melodrama and the woman's film, identified as genres through the standardised Film Studies account. Gay filmmakers like Fassbinder, Waters, Almodóvar, Haynes and Ozon as we have seen, have been especially drawn to melodrama as a form. This is doubly ironic, given that the 1950s Hollywood melodrama, as identified through Film Studies, is a particular type of cinema that assiduously and consistently excluded the possibility of either homosexuality or gay desire as a narrative focus. In fact, homosexuality in the 1950s melodrama becomes perhaps the most conspicuously absent of discourses of sexuality, in a cinema that as Klinger has observed repeatedly addressed 'adult' themes. It seems odd then that gay filmmakers at the end of the twentieth century should so frequently recourse to what might be seen as a rather anachronistic dramatic or stylistic register. One explanation for this paradoxical choice might be the popular contemporary taste for the self-reflexive and ironic, epitomised by Klinger's notion of 'mass camp': melodramatic, 'over the top' narratives and stylistic techniques draw attention in a parodic sense to the artificial construction of gender roles and the norms of heterosexual romance. Another explanation might be that openly gay filmmakers entering the mainstream of culture have to use a recognisable, if anachronistic, rhetoric to situate gay desire because wider heterosexual culture has neither a visual or emotional language to adequately articulate gay desire, existing as it still does outside of societal norms. It might also be as Jane

Shattuc argues that melodrama's lowly status within wider discourses around culture means that it is particularly well suited to gay reappropriation either though camp humour or as a vehicle for the expression of a gay sensibility. Whatever the answer to this question may be it indicates that far from being a redundant mode of expression, melodrama still has the power to move audiences through its ability to convey charged emotional states and moral dilemmas. Melodrama's ability to speak louder, and more eloquently, than words is perhaps the true reason why it remains relevant to critics, filmmakers and audiences alike.

CONCLUSION: IT ALWAYS ENDS IN TEARS

One important thing to emerge from this book is the impact the director Douglas Sirk has had on generations of filmmakers and film scholars. We have seen how the Film Studies debate on melodrama was stimulated (in part, at least) by a reappraisal of Sirk's work and that the initial discussions were concentrated on a relatively small number of his films produced at Universal Studios during the 1950s. These formed the basis of the 'Hollywood family melodrama' as defined by film scholars such as Thomas Elsaesser, Laura Mulvey, Paul Willeman, Fred Camper, Chuck Kleinhans and Thomas Schatz. However, as we have also seen, this was merely the starting point for the study of melodrama. Increasingly the debate has drawn on a wider and much more diverse canon, to the extent that by the 1990s it was being argued that melodrama includes male action movies as much as 'woman's weepies' and domestic dramas. By this time, melodrama was understood to be (as Christine Gledhill and Linda Williams argue) the most pervasive mode of American cinema rather than merely a particular branch of it.

The revision of melodrama within Film Studies that took place from the mid-1980s onwards has extended its scope beyond genre to encompass many (indeed most) genres. Nevertheless, it is clear that a certain conception of melodrama as a more narrowly defined category of cinema (that is, a genre or a small number of closely related genres) still persists within the spheres of film education, film journalism and in the film industry, even within society more generally. The account of melodrama that emerged within Film Studies during the 1970s and early 1980s has established itself firmly within the critical and cultural consciousness.

Consequently there is a widespread presumption that 'melodrama' refers to a set of films that deal with highly-charged emotional issues, characterised by an extravagantly dramatic register and an overtly emotional form of address. In the popular mind, the 1950s films of Douglas Sirk remain the epitomé of this style of cinema. Therefore, his style has been the most emulated, parodied and quoted by successive generations of filmmakers in Hollywood and Europe. It has also inspired and found favour with generations of film students, including ourselves. As university students, we both encountered Sirk's 1950s productions on our film courses. Our teachers valued them and presented them to us as classic examples of Hollywood melodrama. They had a powerful effect upon our hearts and minds, stimulating an abiding fascination that has never diminished and provoked our continued exploration of this area of film in terms of research and teaching. Years later we both find that our university students respond enthusiastically to these same films, consistently choosing them as their examples of classic Hollywood melodrama, producing detailed (and often loving) analyses. It is almost unthinkable that a film course, festival or book on melodrama would not include *All That Heaven Allows, Written on the Wind* or *Imitation of Life*. We certainly could not have imagined writing this book without reference to them, nor had we any doubt that the cover should be a still from one of these movies.

Yet we also understand that Sirk's 1950s Hollywood films are not the be all and end all of melodrama and that good and convincing arguments have been made for why we should look further afield to investigate the operations and effects of melodramatic cinema. As we have described in this book, the debate on melodrama may have begun with a critical engagement with Sirk's films but it very swiftly moved into a larger arena. As the notion of the 'Hollywood family melodrama' was being established, the films of Sirk's contemporaries were included. At the same time, the melodramatic field was traced back to the great silent features of the 1920s and to the films of the 1930s and 1940s, initially associated with Hollywood's films for women but then absorbing films of action, chiefly film noir and crime thrillers but also westerns. Finally, in more recent years, there has been an even more radical expansion of this canon to incorporate the work of Hollywood directors such as Stephen Spielberg. At the same time, the study of melodrama has moved beyond Hollywood (even North America), to include not only British cinema but also the commercial Hindi cinema ('Bollywood'), Chinese cinema and even post-war European art cinema (see the filmography for further details).

We recognise, however, that the dramatic expansion of what is understood as melodrama (shifting from genre to more fluid forms such as style, mode, rhetoric, aesthetic, sensibility) makes this a potentially confusing area of film scholarship. Nevertheless, we also recognise that this has the potential to make melodrama more relevant as a critical tool. Students working in almost every aspect of film are likely to encounter the rhetoric of melodrama operating to greater or lesser extent. This could be in relation to a musical (Hollywood or Bollywood), a western (Hollywood or Spaghetti), in relation to a romantic comedy or a British heritage film. Some scholars and some students of film will embrace this opportunity to rethink established generic categories and investigate the deeper structural levels of films that exist across virtually all genres. In such instances, the expanded notion of melodrama as a mode will be used to examine a more heterogeneous group of films in relation to each other. Others though may continue to cling on to a more established notion of melodrama as a genre or cluster of closely related genres and sub-genres.

Melodrama has always provoked strong emotions, not just from audiences but also from film scholars and critics. We have seen how highly charged the debate on melodrama has been within Film Studies. This has entailed an initial conflict between *mise-en-scène* critics (such as Thomas Elsaesser and Geoffrey Nowell-Smith) and feminist film critics (including Laura Mulvey, Christine Gledhill and Mary Ann Doane) and a later conflict between genre critics (namely, Steve Neale and Rick Altman). No doubt melodrama will remain a contested area of Film Studies, providing an ever-expanding arena in which these battles can be fought out. As film students, we are all able to take up a position within this arena, to take sides or, alternatively, to attempt to arbitrate between the warring factions. Remembering that the tendency within melodrama is towards polarised conflict, if we embark upon this task as students of film, we should steel ourselves to face the sound and fury of our antagonists. Moreover, we should know from the outset that we are likely to fall victim to misunderstanding, even misrepresentation: that it could be a long time before the truth and value our position is publicly recognised and that, in the meantime, many tears will have to be shed. In the end, we may not get all we desire out of such a project but we may at least get something. So, to put it more melodramatically (as Bette Davis does at the end of *Now, Voyager*), 'don't let's ask for the moon, we have the stars!'

NOTES

Introduction

1   Journals include *Film Score Monthly, Music From the Movies* and *Soundtrack!*. Web sites include www.filmsound.org/filmmusic, www.filmmusic.com, www. filmscoremonthly.com, and www.celluloidtunes.com.

2   Kassabian (2001) also discusses this problem p 9–10.

3   Examples include *Blue Velvet* (1986), *Pretty in Pink* (1986), *Stand By Me* (1986), *Pretty Woman* (1990) and *Boys Don't Cry* (1999).

4   The Dogme 95 'Vow of Chastity' states that music must not be used unless it occurs where the scene is shot.

Chapter one

1   See Linda Williams' section on Griffith in her chapter 'Melodrama Revised' in Nick Browne (ed.) *Refiguring American Film Genres*. Berkeley: University of California Press, 1998, 62–82.

2   For more detailed discussion of British and Indian forms of film melodrama, see Sue Harper's essay 'Historical Pleasures: Gainsborough Costume Melodrama', in Christine Gledhill (ed.) (1987) *Home is Where the Heart Is*. London: BFI, 167–96; and Ravi Vasudevan's 'The Melodramatic Mode and the Commercial Hindi Cinema', *Screen*, 30, 3, 1989, 29–50.

3   At the same time, of course, other features (namely their differences) are ignored. Analysing these three films in relation to the model described above ignores these differences to the point where Griffiths' silent drama of domes-

tic violence and racial prejudice becomes conflated with both a maternal melodrama (and woman's film) and a juvenile delinquency film.

4   For a fuller discussion see 'Tales of Sound and Fury,' *Monogram*, 4, 1972, 2–15, reprinted in Christine Gledhill's book of edited essays, *Home is Where the Heart Is: Studies in Melodrama and the Woman's Film*. London: British Film Institute, 1987, 43–69.

5   See Jackie Stacey (1994) *Star Gazing: Hollywood Cinema and Female Spectatorship*. London: Routledge.

6   See Janet Staiger (1992) *Interpreting Films: Studies in the Historical Reception of American Cinema*. Princeton: Princeton University Press.

7   See Jeanine Basinger (1993) *A Woman's View: How Hollywood Spoke to Women 1930–1960*. London: Chatto & Windus.

8   See Ben Singer (1990) 'Female Power in the Serial Queen Melodrama', *Camera Obscura* 22, January, 90–129.

9   *Now, Voyager* is the tale of Charlotte Vale (Bette Davis), an unattractive, sexually-repressed spinster on the verge of a nervous breakdown, who is the victim of a domineering mother (Gladys Cooper). She is ultimately saved and restored to health, mental well-being and beauty by a psychiatrist (Claude Rains), a well-meaning cousin (Ilka Chase) and a handsome European lover (Paul Henreid). Tragedy and romance provide the essential ingredients in this woman's journey to adult identity, self-determination and personal fulfilment. Her encounters with her psychiatrist and lover give her hope, strength and confidence, whilst her mother consistently (even after death) throws her back into neurotic insecurity, illness and despair. Becoming a surrogate mother to her lover's child offers Charlotte the best prospect of fulfilment and stability. However, this can only be achieved through an extraordinary act of personal sacrifice, by giving up her love affair.

10 See the description of this film in chapter three.

11 *The Wild One* featured a young Marlon Brando as the leader of a motorcycle gang hell-bent on terrorising a local community.

Chapter two

1   Sirk's father was indeed born in Denmark but had become a German national.

2   *Magnificent Obsession* was Universal's biggest success in 1954. Jane Wyman was Oscar-nominated for *All That Heaven Allows* as was Robert Stack for *Written on the Wind*, Dorothy Malone gained an Oscar for the same film. *Imitation of Life* also gained Oscar nominations and awards for Susan Kohner and Juanita Moore and was Universal's most successful film ever.

3   Barbara Klinger discusses the targeting of female consumers during the 1950s in more detail than is possible here in her book *Melodrama and Meaning*.

4   The original *Imitation of Life* was made in 1934 starring Claudette Colbert.

5   For Brecht the dominant mode of theatrical realism was a bourgeois concept concerned with justifying the ways things were rather than the way things should be. Brecht did not, as is sometimes argued, reject realism out of hand – he called for a different kind of realism in the theatre that was not about maintaining the status quo but about questioning the conditions of human existence. He wrote extensively about his dramatic philosophies and in *Appendices to the Short Organum* he outlines his views on realism explicitly: 'The bourgeois theatre's performances always aim at smoothing over contradictions, at creating false harmony, at idealisation. Conditions are reported as if they could not be otherwise ... None of this is like reality, so a realistic theatre must give it up' (1964: 277).

6   Sirk gave a rare televised interview in 1979 for the BBC *Arena* documentary profile of his life and career, *Behind the Mirror: A Profile of Douglas Sirk*.

Chapter three

1   The classic realist text here refers to those forms of cinema (such as the Classical Hollywood film) which erase all traces of their construction in order to create the appearance of an unmediated message by using the techniques of continuity editing (shot/reverse shot, eyeline matches, matches on action, and so on).

2   We should maybe add a sixth feature here, that of the central role played by the villain as the motivator of the plot and primary source of excitement, who defies the conventions and taboos which the rest of the characters (and probably the audience too) live by.

FILMOGRAPHY

The films listed here should not be regarded as a comprehensive list of melodrama films. They are more a selection of useful and readily available films that illustrate many of the themes, stylistic conventions and narrative concerns that have been discussed in this book.

For ease of reference the films are listed thematically and wherever possible contemporary as well as Classical Hollywood examples have been provided. This list of films has been chosen to illustrate the different ways of conceiving of melodrama. All the films have a high quotient of pathos, organising the audience's knowledge, point of view and sympathy in such a way as to provoke tears.

Many of these films focus on characters whose moral virtue (their innate goodness) or innocence is not recognised by anyone other than the audience until the narrative climax. Some of these films are aimed specifically at female audiences, whilst others primarily address male spectators. Mostly though they are aimed at mixed audiences of males and females. Some of these films use realistic aesthetics (in terms of iconography, cinematography, editing, dialogue and performance), even 'Neo-Realism' and *cinema vérité*. Others use fantasy (make-believe) to create new realities (for example, science fiction) although even here realist aesthetics are still used to make these credible (as possible worlds) and still have strong and clear connections to everyday life. Some of these films use a high level of comedy to offset the pathos, enabling the audience's emotions to shift back and forth from the extremes of laughter and tears, as means of releasing pent-up emotion. Others have a high level of action, again to express and release emotional tension. Laughter, tears and prolonged action sequences are a means of catharsis in melodrama and the films included in this list employ one or other (or all) of these to release the tension that has otherwise been built up.

In virtually all the films cited here, music is used to heighten, orchestrate and punctuate the audience's emotional response. Some are, in fact, musicals. Films are drawn from a broad range of generic categories (mostly following the categories used by critics, reviewers and journalists). Along with musicals, there are war films, westerns, crime films, film noir, psychological dramas, historical costume dramas, family melodramas, maternal melodramas, juvenile delinquency films, queer cinema, AIDS movies, action movies, heritage cinema and European art cinema.

Whilst sharing qualities with other films in their generic groupings, the films listed here all share properties with each other, constituting a broad and diverse mode of mainstream narrative cinema. More work is no doubt required to fully identify and understand the properties that link all of these films together.

SIRK'S UNIVERSAL MELODRAMAS
All I Desire (Douglas Sirk, 1953)
All That Heaven Allows (Douglas Sirk, 1956)
Imitation of Life (Douglas Sirk, 1959)
Interlude (Douglas Sirk, 1957)
Magnificent Obsession (Douglas Sirk, 1954)
The Tarnished Angels (Douglas Sirk, 1958)
There's Always Tomorrow (Douglas Sirk, 1956)
Written on the Wind (Douglas Sirk, 1956)

'SIRKIAN' MELODRAMAS
Far From Heaven (Todd Haynes, 2002)
Fear Eats the Soul (Rainer Werner Fassbinder, 1974)
The Flower of My Secret (Pedro Almodóvar, 1995)
The Merchant of Four Seasons (Rainer Werner Fassbinder, 1972)
Polyester (John Waters, 1981)

THE WOMAN'S FILM
Autumn Leaves (Robert Aldrich, 1956)
Beaches (Garry Marshall, 1988)
Beyond the Forest (King Vidor, 1949)

Breaking the Waves (Lars von Trier, 1996)
The Bridges of Madison County (Clint Eastwood, 1995)
Camille (George Cukor, 1936)
Come Back to the Five and Dime, Jimmy Dean, Jimmy Dean
　　(Robert Altman, 1983)
Dark Victory (Edmund Goulding, 1939)
Delores Claiborne (Taylor Hackford, 1995)
The Hours (Stephen Daldry, 2002)
I'll Cry Tomorrow (Daniel Mann 1955)
I Want to Live! (Robert Mann, 1958)
Johnny Belinda (Jean Negulesco, 1948)
Julia (Fred Zinnemann, 1977)
Letter From an Unknown Woman (Max Ophuls, 1948)
Moonstruck (Norman Jewison, 1987)
Now Voyager (Irving Rapper, 1942)
Places in the Heart (Robert Benton, 1984)
Random Harvest (Mervyn Le Roy, 1942)
Stella Dallas (King Vidor, 1937)
Terms of Endearment (James L. Brooks, 1983)
Yanks (John Schlesinger, 1979)

ROMANCE/DOOMED LOVE
Anna Karenina (Clarence Brown, 1935)
Duel in the Sun (King Vidor, 1946)
Gone With the Wind (Victor Flemming, 1939)
Love is a Many Splendoured Thing (Henry King, 1955)
Love Story (Arthur Hiller, 1970)
Waterloo Bridge (Mervyn LeRoy, 1940)
The Way We Were (Sydney Pollack, 1973)
Wuthering Heights (William Wyler, 1939)

FAMILY MELODRAMAS
Cat on a Hot Tin Roof (Richard Brooks, 1958)
Festen (Thomas Vinterberg, 1998)
Giant (George Stevens, 1956)
The Graduate (Mike Nichols, 1967)
Home From the Hill (Vincente Minnelli, 1960)
King's Row (Sam Wood, 1941)
On Golden Pond (Mark Rydall, 1981)

Peyton Place (Mark Robson, 1957)
Picnic (Joshua Logan, 1955)
Ordinary People (Robert Redford, 1980)
Who's Afraid of Virginia Woolf? (Mike Nichols, 1966)

THE MALE MELODRAMA I: THE MALE WEEPIE
Best Years of Our Lives (William Wyler, 1946)
Bigger Than Life (Nicholas Ray, 1956)
The Champ (Franco Zeffirelli, 1979)
Citizen Kane (Orsen Welles, 1941)
Dead Poet's Society (Peter Weir, 1989)
East of Eden (Elia Kazan, 1955)
Field of Dreams (Phil Alden Robinson, 1989)
It's a Wonderful Life (Frank Capra, 1947)
Some Came Running (Vincente Minnelli, 1958)
Rebel Without a Cause (Nicholas Ray, 1955)
Regarding Henry (Mike Nichols, 1991)

THE MALE MELODRAMA II: THE ACTION MELODRAMA
Braveheart (Mel Gibson, 1995)
Deliverance (John Boorman, 1972)
Die Hard (John McTiernan, 1988)
Gladiator (Ridley Scott, 2000)
Predator (John McTiernan, 1987)
Rambo: First Blood II (George P. Cosmatos, 1985)
Rocky (John G. Avildsen, 1976)

MATERNAL MELODRAMAS
Stella Dallas (King Vidor, 1936)
Madame X (David Lowell Rich, 1965)
The Old Maid (Edmund Goudling, 1939)
Only Yesterday (John Stahl, 1933)
To Each His Own (Mitchell Leisen, 1946)

MUSICAL MELODRAMAS
Cabaret (Bob Fosse, 1972)
Camelot (Joshua Logan, 1967)
Carousel (Henry King, 1956)
Dancer in the Dark (Lars von Trier, 2000)

Dirty Dancing (Emile Ardolino, 1987)
The King and I (Walter Lang, 1956)
Meet Me in St Louis (Vincente Minnelli, 1944)
Saturday Night Fever (John Badham, 1978)
The Sound of Music (Robert Wise, 1965)
A Star is Born (George Cukor, 1954)
West Side Story (Robert Wise, 1961)
Yentl (Barbra Streisand, 1983)

SILENT MELODRAMA
Broken Blossoms (D. W. Griffiths, 1919)
City Lights (Charles Chaplin, 1931)
Greed (Erich von Stroheim, 1923)
Orphans of the Storm (D. W. Griffiths, 1921)
The Sheik (George Melford, 1921)
Sunrise (F. W. Murnau, 1927)
Way Down East (D. W. Griffiths, 1920)
The Wind (Victor Sjorstrom, 1928)

WAR FILMS
The Big Parade (King Vidor, 1925)
The Four Horsemen of the Apocalypse (Rex Ingram, 1921)
In Which We Serve (Noel Coward and David Lean, 1942)
Life is Beautiful (Roberto Benigni, 1997)
Millions Like Us (Frank Launder and Sidney Gilliat, 1943)
Mrs Miniver (William Wyler, 1942)
Schindler's List (Steven Spielberg, 1993)
Since You Went Away (John Cromwell, 1944)
Watch on the Rhine (Herman Shulmin, 1943)

GAINSBOROUGH MELODRAMA
Caravan (Arthur Crabtree, 1946)
Fanny by Gaslight (Anthony Asquith, 1944)
Jassy (Bernard Knowles, 1947)
Love Story (Leslie Arliss, 1944)
Madonna of the Seven Moons (Arthur Crabtree, 1944)
The Man in Grey (Leslie Arliss, 1943)
They Were Sisters (Arthur Crabtree, 1945)
The Wicked Lady (Leslie Arlis, 1945)

HISTORICAL COSTUME MELODRAMAS
All This and Heaven Too (Anatole Litvak, 1940)
The Color Purple (Steven Spielberg, 1984)
Dangerous Liaisons (Stephen Frears, 1988)
Gone to Earth (Michael Powell and Emeric Pressburger, 1950)
Jane Eyre (Robert Stevenson, 1943)
Jezebel (William Wyler, 1938)
Madame Bovary (Vincente Minelli, 1949)
The Private Lives of Elizabeth and Essex (Michael Curtiz, 1939)

AIDS, GAY, LESBIAN AND QUEER CINEMA
Boys Don't Cry (Kimberley Peirce, 1999)
The Crying Game (Neil Jordan, 1992)
Death in Venice (Luchino Visconti, 1971)
Desert Hearts (Donna Deitch, 1985)
Fried Green Tomatos (Jon Avnet, 1991)
Kiss of the Spider Woman (Hector Babenco, 1985)
Longtime Companion (Norman Rene, 1990)
Love, Valor, Compassion (Joe Mantello, 1997)
Maurice (James Ivory, 1987)
My Beautiful Launderette (Stephen Frears, 1985)
Philadelphia (Jonathan Demme, 1993)
Salmonberries (Percy Adlon, 1991)
Tea and Sympathy (Vincente Minnelli, 1956)
Torch Song Trilogy (Paul Bogart, 1988)

FILM NOIR
The Big Sleep (Hward Hawks, 1946)
Caught (Max Ophuls, 1948)
Crossfire (Edward Dmytryk, 1947)
Deception (Irving Rapper, 1947)
Double Indemnity (Billy Wilder, 1944)
Gilda (Charles Vidor, 1946)
Humoresque (Jean Negulesco, 1947)
Kiss Me Deadly (Robert Aldrich, 1955)
Laura (Otto Preminger, 1944)
Mildred Pierce (Michael Curtiz, 1945)
The Postman Always Rings Twice (Tay Garnett, 1946)
Sunset Boulevard (Billy Wilder, 1950)

WESTERN MELODRAMAS
Drums Along the Mohawk (John Ford, 1939)
Johnny Guitar (Nicholas Ray, 1953)
A Man Called Horse (Elliott Silverstein, 1970)
Rancho Notorious (Fritz Lang, 1952)
River of No Return (Otto Preminger, 1954)
Shane (George Stevens, 1953)
Stagecoach (John Ford, 1939)
Walk on the Wild Side (Edward Dmytryk, 1962)

PYCHOLOGICAL MELODRAMA
Baby Doll (Elia Kazan, 1956)
Black Narcissus (Michael Powell and Emeric Pressburger, 1947)
The Dark Mirror (Robert Siodmak, 1946)
Marnie (Alfred Hitchcock, 1964)
Nuts (Martin Ritt, 1987)
One Flew Over the Cuckoo's Nest (Milos Forman, 1975)
Possessed (Curtis Bernhardt, 1947)
Psycho (Alfred Hitchcock, 1960)
Spellbound (Alfred Hitchcock, 1945)
Suddenly Last Summer (Joseph L. Mankiewicz, 1959)
Vertigo (Alfred Hitchcock, 1958)

BRITISH MELODRAMA
Angela's Ashes (Alan Parker, 1999)
Billy Elliott (Stephen Daldry, 2000)
Brief Encounter (David Lean, 1945)
Dance with a Stranger (Mike Newell, 1985)
Distant Voices, Still Lives (Terence Davies, 1988)
Dr. Zhivago (David Lean, 1965)
I Know Where I'm Going (Michael Powell and Emeric Pressburger, 1945)
It Always Rains on Sunday (Robert Hamer, 1947)
Mandy (Alexander Mackendrick, 1952)
The Spanish Gardener (Philip Leacock, 1956)
Thief of Bagdad (Michael Powell, 1940)
That Hamilton Woman (Alexander Korda, 1941)
Yield to the Night (J. Lee Thompson, 1956)

'BOLLYWOOD' MELODRAMA
Asoka (Santosh Sivan, 2001)
Devdas (Bimal Roy, 1955)
Devdas (Sanjay Leela Bhansali, 2002)
Kabhi Kabhie (Yash Chopra, 1976)
Pakeezah (Kamal Amrohi, 1971)
Sholay (Ramesh Sippy, 1975)
Umrao Jaan (Muzaffar Ali, 1981)

CHINESE MELODRAMA
Crouching Tiger, Hidden Dragon (Ang Lee, 2000)
Farewell My Concubine (Chen Kaige, 1993)
Ju-Dou (Yang Fengliang and Zhang Yimou, 1990)
Raise the Red Lantern (Zhang Yimou, 1991)
Shanghai Triad (Zhang Yimou, 1995)
The Story of Qiu Ju (Zhang Yimou, 1992)
Temptress Moon (Chen Kaige, 1996)
To Live (Zhang Yimou, 1994)

EUROPEAN MELODRAMA
Autumn Sonata (Ingmar Bergman, 1978)
Cries and Whispers (Ingmar Bergman, 1972)
Les Dammes du Bois de Boulogne (Robert Bresson, 1954)
The Damned (Luchino Visconti, 1969)
L'Innocente (Luchino Visconti, 1976)
The Passion of Anna (Ingmar Bergman, 1969)
Persona (Ingmar Bergman, 1966)
Senso (Luchino Visconti, 1954)

BIBLIOGRAPHY

SELECT READING LIST

This list includes some of the most useful Film Studies texts on melodrama that are currently available along with brief descriptions of their contents.

Peter Brooks (1976) *The Melodramatic Imagination: Balzac, Henry James, Melodrama and the Mode of Excess*. New Haven: Yale University Press.
Though this is a work of literary criticism and only mentions Film Studies in the revised preface to the 1995 edition it is nonetheless an extremely useful book for a clear understanding of the theatrical traditions of melodrama. In the first half of the book Brooks identifies the narrative and stylistic techniques of mostly French theatrical melodrama and in the second half he discusses the ways in which these patterns are drawn upon in the work of nineteenth-century novelists. Brooks' work is important because he identifies melodrama as an excessive mode used to articulate moral conflicts in both theatre and literature which he argues is an expression of a modern sensibility, shifting away from faith in a divine order to a new preoccupation with what he describes as the 'moral occult'. Brooks' work has been extremely influential in redefining debate around melodrama in Film Studies, especially in terms of thinking of melodrama as a modality in cinema.

Christine Gledhill (ed.) (1987) *Home is Where the Heart Is: Studies in Melodrama and the Woman's Film*. London: British Film Institute.
A classic Film Studies reader on melodrama, Gledhill's collection remains the most comprehensive collection of important essays on the subject. Including

Thomas Elsaesser's key work, 'Tales of Sound and Fury', as well as work by Laura Mulvey, Geoffrey Nowell-Smith, David Rodowick, Anette Kuhn, Tania Modleski, Linda Williams and Mary Ann Doane, *Home is Where the Heart Is*, whilst published in 1987, continues to be essential reading for Film Studies students as it charts the concerns and interests of a range of approaches to melodrama and the ways in which the connection between melodrama and the woman's film have been established. There are a few conspicuous absences in this overview however, notably Paul Willemen's essays on Douglas Sirk, Fassbinder's useful commentaries as well as the auteurist approach of Fred Camper. Gledhill's own lengthy introduction to the collection is one of the most cogent and perceptive overviews of melodrama as a critical field currently in print.

Jon Halliday (1971, reprinted 1997) *Sirk on Sirk: Conversations with Jon Halliday*. London: Faber & Faber.

Jon Halliday's interview with the retired Douglas Sirk played an important part in construction of the Film Studies account of the family melodrama. *Sirk on Sirk* covers the whole of the director's career, starting with his experiences in Weimar theatre, through his early films for UFA and to his eventual departure for Hollywood. The book is useful background reading and illustrates very clearly Sirk's intellectual approach to film making based on his academic background in art history. It also vividly demonstrates the important role that Sirk played in the revision of his cinema, especially the construction of Sirk as a progressive and subversive critic of Eisenhower's America. Chapter 5, dealing with the period from 1950 to 1959 and the conditions of production during his years as a contract director at Universal, is the most useful section for students of cinematic melodrama.

Barbara Klinger (1994) *Melodrama and Meaning: History, Culture and the Films of Douglas Sirk*. Bloomington: Indiana University Press.

Barbara Klinger's excellent study of the shifting reception of Douglas Sirk's films is an immensely readable and thorough analysis of the differing ways in which his films have been understood by academics, journalists and audiences. Klinger argues that the meaning of any cinematic text cannot be fixed but needs to be understood in a wider social, cultural and historical context. She notes that Sirk's films were appropriated by Film Studies as examples of the so called 'progressive text', were sold to cinemagoers as daring films with adult themes of affluence and sexuality and can be read by contemporary audiences as examples of anachronistic camp excess.

Jane Shattuc (1995) *Television, Tabloids, and Tears: Fassbinder and Popular Culture.* Minneapolis: University of Minnesota Press.
Like Klinger's study of Douglas Sirk, Jane Shattuc's work on Fassbinder is primarily a reception study. Shattuc places Fassbinder as a central figure in the German counterculture movement of the late 1960s and illustrates the ways in which scandalised press reports of his private life fed into the popular reception of his films. The study argues that melodrama was a dramatic strategy essential to not only the understanding of Fassbinder's films but also to the ways in which his public persona was constructed. The book provides detailed background information concerning the political and social context in which Fassbinder emerged in Germany, discusses his relationship with experimental theatre and the much discussed influence of Sirk in his films.

FULLER BIBLIOGRAPHY

Altman, R. (1981) *Genre: The Musical.* London: British Film Institute.
_____ (1987) *The American Film Musical.* London, Bloomington and Indianopolis: British Film Institute and Indiana University Press.
_____ (1998) 'Reusable Packaging: Generic Products and the Recycling Process', in Nick Browne (ed.) *Refiguring American Film Genres: History and Theory.* Berkeley: University of California Press, 1–41.
Artaud, A. (2001) *The Theatre and its Double.* London: Calder Publications.
Basinger, J. (1993) *A Woman's View: How Hollywood Spoke to Women 1930–1960.* London: Chatto & Windus.
Brecht, B. (1964) *Brecht on Theatre: The Development of an Aesthetic.* London: Methuen.
Browne, N. (ed.) (1998) *Refiguring American Film Genres: History and Theory.* Berkeley: University of California Press.
Browne, N., P. G. Pickowicz, V. Sobchack and E. Yau (eds) (1994) *New Chinese Cinemas: Forms, Identities, Politics.* Cambridge: Cambridge University Press.
Butler, A. (2002) *Women's Cinema: The Contested Screen.* London: Wallflower Press.
Byars, J. (1991) *All That Hollywood Allows: Re-reading Gender in 1950s Melodrama.* London: Routledge.
Camper, F. (1971) 'The Films of Douglas Sirk', *Screen*, 12, 2, 44–62.
Cohan, S. (1997) *Masked Men: Masculinity and the Movies in the Fifties.* Bloomington: Indiana University Press.
Cook, P. (ed.) (1984) *The Cinema Book.* London: British Film Institute.
Cook, P. (1991) 'Melodrama and the Women's Picture', in M. Landy (ed.) *Imitations*

of Life: A Reader on Film and Television Melodrama. Detroit: Wayne State University Press.

Creed, B. (1977) 'The Position of Women in Hollywood Melodramas', *Australian Journal of Screen Theory*, 4, 27–31.

Dyer, R, (1990) *Now You See It: Studies on Lesbian and Gay Cinema.* London: Routledge.

Doane, M. A. (1987) *The Desire to Desire: The Woman's Film of the 1940s.* London: Macmillan.

Elsaesser, T. (1972) 'Tales of Sound and Fury: Observations on the Family Melodrama', in C. Gledhill (ed.) (1987) *Home is Where the Heart is: Studies in Melodrama and the Woman's Film.* London: British Film Institute, 43–69.

Fassbinder, R. W. (1992) *The Anarchy of the Imagination: Interviews, Essays, Notes.* Baltimore: Johns Hopkins University Press.

Feuer, J. (1984) 'Melodrama, Serial Form and Television Today', *Screen*, 25, 1, 4–16.

Fletcher, J. (1988a?) 'Versions of Masquerade', *Screen*, 29, 3, 43–70.

_____ (1988b?) 'Melodrama: An Introduction.' *Screen*, 29, 3, 2–12.

Gibbs, J. (2002) *Mise-en-scène: Film Style and Interpretation.* London: Wallflower Press.

Gledhill, C. (1986) 'Stella Dallas and Feminist Film Theory', *Cinema Journal*, 25, 4, 44–48.

_____ (1987) 'The Melodramatic Field: An Investigation', in *Home is Where the Heart Is: Studies in Melodrama and the Woman's Film.* London: British Film Institute, 5–39.

Gledhill, C. and L. Williams (eds) (2000) *Reinventing Film Studies.* London: Hodder Arnold.

Hammond, M. (1993) 'The Historical and the Hysterical: Melodrama, War and Masculinity in *Dead Poet's Society*', in P. Kirkham (ed.) *You Tarzan: Masculinities, Movies and Men.* London: Lawrence & Wishart.

Haskell, M. (1974) *From Reverence to Rape* (2nd edn.). Chicago and London: University of Chicago Press.

Jeffords, S. (1994) *Hard Bodies: Hollywood Masculinity in the Regan Era.* New York: Rutgers University Press.

Kleinhans, C. (1978) 'Notes on Melodrama and the Family Under Capitalism,' *Film Reader 3*, 40–47.

Klinger, B. (1986) 'Cinema/Ideology/Criticism Revisited – The Progressive Text', *Screen*, 25, 1, 30–44.

Krutnik, F. (1991) *In a Lonely Street: 'Film Noir', Genre, Masculinity.* London: Routledge.

Kuhn, A. (1984) 'Women's Genres', *Screen*, 25, 1, 18–28.

Merritt, R. (1993) 'Melodrama, Postmortem for a Phantom Genre,' in *Wide Angle*, 5, 3, 24–31.

Morse, D. (1972) 'Aspects of Melodrama', *Monogram*, 4, 16–17.

Mulvey, L. (1975) 'Visual Pleasure and Narrative Cinema', *Screen*, 16, 3, 6–18.

____ (1977/78) 'Notes on Sirk and Melodrama', *Movie*, 25, Winter, 53–6.

Neale, S. (1986) 'Melodrama and Tears', *Screen*, 27, 6, 6–22.

____ (1993) 'Melo Talk: On the Meaning and Use of the Term "Melodrama" in the American Trade Press', *Velvet Light Trap*, Fall, 66–89.

____ (2000) *Genre and Hollywood*. Londona and New York: Routledge.

Nichols, B. (ed.) (1976) *Movies and Methods Vol. I*. Berkeley: University of California Press.

Nowell-Smith, G. (1977) 'Minnelli and Melodrama', *Screen,* 18, 2, 113–19.

Pollock, G. (1977) 'Report on the Weekend School' *Screen*, 18, 2, 105–13.

Quart, L. & A. Auster (1984) *American Film and Society Since 1945*. London,: Macmillan.

Schatz, T. (1981) *Hollywood Genres: Formulas, Filmmaking and the Studio System*. Philadelphia: Temple University Press.

Singer, B. (1990) 'Female Power in the Serial Queen Melodrama', *Camera Obscura*, 22, 90–129.

Stacey, J. (1994) *Star Gazing*. London: Routledge.

Staiger, J. (1992) *Interpreting Films: Studies in the Historical Reception of American Cinema*. Princeton: Princeton University Press.

Thompson, K. (1999) 'The Concept of Cinematic Excess', in L. Braudy and M. Cohen (eds) *Film Theory and Criticism: Introductory Readings*. Oxford: Oxford University Press.

Vasudevan, R. (1989) 'The Melodramatic Mode in the Commercial Hindi Cinema', *Screen*, 30, 3, 29–50.

Willemen, P. (1971) 'Notes on the Sirkian System', *Screen*, 12, 2, 63–7.

____ (1972) 'Towards an Analysis of the Sirkian System', *Screen*, 13, 4, 128–34.

Williams, L. (1998) 'Melodrama Revisited', in N. Browne (ed.) *Refiguring American Film Genres: History and Theory*. Berkeley: University of California Press.

INDEX

CPSIA information can be obtained
at www.ICGtesting.com
Printed in the USA
LVHW110118221222
735707LV00004B/640

9 781904 764021